KILLING THE
DEEP STATE

KILLING THE DEEP STATE

The Fight to Save President Trump

JEROME R. CORSI, PhD

Humanix Books

www.humanixbooks.com

Humanix Books

Killing the Deep State
Copyright © 2018 by Jerome R. Corsi
All rights reserved

Humanix Books, P.O. Box 20989, West Palm Beach, FL 33416, USA
www.humanixbooks.com | info@humanixbooks.com

Library of Congress Cataloging-in-Publication Data is available upon request.

Humanix Books is a division of Humanix Publishing, LLC. Its trademark, consisting of the word "Humanix," is registered in the Patent and Trademark Office and in other countries.

ISBN: 978-1-63006-102-9 (Hardcover)
ISBN: 978-163006-103-6 (E-book)

Printed in the United States of America
10 9 8 7 6 5 4 3 2 1

Contents

           Trump from Office   77

   7   The Trump Dossier   79

   8   The Truth about "Russian Collusion"   97

   9   Mainstream Media Attack Trump   119

  10   Antifa Anarchists Go Wild   133

Part 3   **How Trump Wins**   143

  11   How Trump Can Win the Propaganda War   145

  12   The Counteroffensive Trump Must Launch   159

       Conclusion: The Fight to Save President Trump   175

       Notes   189

       Index   217

Introduction

You know, to just be grossly generalistic, you could put half of Trump's supporters into what I call the "basket of deplorables."

—Hillary Clinton, September 9, 2016

ON JULY 26, 2017, UNDER a search warrant obtained by Special Prosecutor Robert Mueller, the FBI conducted a predawn raid on the Alexandria, Virginia, home of former Trump campaign aide Paul Manafort, even though Manafort had testified voluntarily to the Senate Intelligence Committee on July 25 and was cooperating fully with the special counselor's investigation into the Trump campaign's collusion with Russia.

At Mueller's instruction, the FBI picked the lock of Manafort's front door and burst into his home while he and his wife were sleeping. This raid smacked of government prosecutorial impropriety, with Mueller using police-state strong-arm tactics to intimidate a target of the investigation. Mueller's intended result was to strike terror not only into the hearts of Manafort and his family but also into the minds and hearts of any Washington operatives still supporting President Donald J. Trump.

Given that Manafort was cooperating with Mueller's investigation, it is likely that the predawn raid yielded documentary evidence that Manafort would have handed over willingly, had the Department of Justice bothered to ask. What the gestapo-like break-in signals is that Mueller, as special counselor, has joined forces with the Democratic Party, the mainstream media, and Deep State intelligence agency operatives who are out to destroy the Trump administration.

In the eyes of the Deep State, Trump dared to suggest during the campaign that the United States could negotiate successfully with Russia and China to combat terrorism, reduce the chance of nuclear war, and negotiate international trade deals that would be fair to the United States. Among Trump's first acts in office was to cancel President Obama's Trans-Pacific Partnership and to pull out of the Obama-negotiated United Nations Paris Climate Accord, two moves certain to threaten international globalists and their central bank financiers.

To win the presidency, Trump defeated 16 GOP establishment contenders, plus Hillary Clinton, the overwhelming first choice of international globalists and central bankers worldwide. To appreciate how threatening Trump's election was to the Deep State, understand that international globalists and their central bank financiers have had a New World Order hold on the White House since Ronald Reagan left office—through four administrations, including the presidencies of George H. W. Bush, Bill Clinton, George W. Bush, and Barack Obama.

Trump won the presidency by defying political correctness and threatening to replace the rule of multinational corporations and borderless international organizations, including both the International Monetary Fund and the World Bank, with a return to a populist form of nationalist economics and politics that vowed to put "America First."

From the moment that Trump surprised pundits across the globe by winning the 2016 presidential election, Deep State activists in the United States vowed that Trump would never be permitted to rule effectively. Joined by GOP elite establishment leaders in Washington, House Speaker Paul Ryan and Senate Majority Leader Mitch McConnell vowed that Trump's legislative agenda would be blocked, despite their public assurances of allegiance to the new president.

The Deep State had been convinced that Hillary would win and that a second Clinton presidency would allow the Deep State to continue running the international drug trade while supporting the military-industrial complex in a policy of perpetual war. With Hillary prepared to confront both Russia and China as enemies, the Deep State felt reassured that central bankers worldwide would continue to fund US military adventures around the globe. Moreover, with Hillary as president, the Deep State could be confident that 2009-like government bailouts would be readily available to keep from exploding the multi-trillion-dollar fiat currency debt bubble that imperils the global economy. With Hillary in the White House, central bankers were confident they could print as much fiat currency as was needed to continue funding perpetual military conflicts without worrying about the doubling of the US national debt experienced during Obama's eight years in office. Multinational corporations could anticipate the expansion of international trade deals without being concerned that Russia and China's competitive advantages would undercut the US by providing readily available cheap labor to government-subsidized commercial operations. Globalists could look forward to continued open borders and a massive influx of Middle Eastern refugees as the US rushed to the finish line of ending US national sovereignty once and for all.

The risk the Deep State faced if Trump actually succeeded in winning the election was the exposure of four traitorous US presidencies. George H. W. Bush, along with Bill Clinton, George W. Bush, and Barack Obama, engineered such criminal travesties as the invasion of Iraq, a "fast-and-furious" gunrunning to the Mexican drug cartels, more illegal gunrunning to Libya and Syria, as well as a plan to support the Muslim Brotherhood's penetration of the top levels of the US national security apparatus, including the White House, the National Security Council, and numerous intelligence agencies, including the CIA.

If Hillary had won, she would have completed the Obama administration's dictatorial decision to weaponize the federal bureaucracy. The losers would be patriots "clinging to their Bibles and their guns," dumb enough to believe even today in the US Constitution and the freedoms our Founding Fathers bequeathed to all subsequent generations of Americans. With the willing complicity of globalists, central bankers, intelligence operatives, and military leaders around the world, Hillary planned to perpetuate the Clinton Foundation for decades to come as a vast criminal enterprise, designed to enrich Bill, Hillary, Chelsea, and their descendants into perpetuity.

As radical socialists in sympathy with Muslim radicals gained control of the Democratic Party, Hillary's 2016 presidential campaign championed a hard-left brand of identity politics. The goal of her "antihate" agenda was to undermine what is left of the American Republic. What Hillary and the hard-left ideology she embraced aimed to destroy was the Judeo-Christian ethics and the free enterprise principles that have been keys to the success of the American experiment.

What is at stake today is not just the presidency of Donald J. Trump but the very survival a United States of America that allows the Constitution and our fundamental freedoms to continue for future generations.

To "kill" the Deep State, Donald J. Trump must defeat Robert Mueller's plan to remove him from office one way or the other— either by impeachment or by declaring him mentally unfit under the terms of the 25th Amendment. To save his presidency, Trump must expose a host of criminally cunning Deep State political operatives as enemies to the Constitution, including John Brennan, Eric Holder, Loretta Lynch, James Comey, and Robert Mueller—as well as Barack Obama and Hillary Clinton.

The NSA spying on the American people must end now. The CIA must finally be "broken up into a thousand pieces," as John F. Kennedy swore in a promise that cost him his life. Trump must not delay in "draining the swamp" at the FBI, the DOJ, and the IRS in addition to the CIA. President Trump must end the Deep State's control of the international drug trade, even if doing so requires legalizing a wide range of drugs that can be controlled as we control alcohol today.

Under the past four presidencies, the United States has been the leading nation competing in the international arms trade. President Trump must make certain that no secretary of state will ever repeat Hillary Clinton's secret plan to use the Department of State as a cover to destabilize nations like Libya or to subsequently run guns illegally through Libya to equip al-Qaeda terrorists fighting in Syria.

President Trump must direct the FBI and the Department of Justice to return to their duly constituted duties of faithfully executing and enforcing laws on the books, including laws regarding illegal immigration.

The bloated bureaucracy with its Clinton and Obama holdovers operates today as a fourth branch of government, enacting its own laws by inventing thousands of rules and regulations. Trump must end this leftist monster, firing bureaucrats by the thousands and closing departments pursuing their own ideological agendas.

Trump must put an end to the Federal Reserve System and its bubble-generating fiat currency before central bankers have time to execute their plan of plunging the global economy into a nightmare of global economic depression. The IRS must be disbanded, as the American people reject both the Federal Reserve system and the income tax as unconstitutional pillars on which Deep State globalists and central bankers depend to finance their evil, unconstitutional shadow government.

While all this will not be accomplished in one year, or perhaps even in one term, President Trump must begin. This is a war Trump can win, even though as in the general election itself, the odds are against him. But to win this war, the "Trump Train" must gain momentum against the Deep State, proving once again that the so-called basket of deplorables are yet a formidable force, capable of defeating even the Deep State's well-established and well-financed traitors.

We patriots must today resolve that we are once again the last, best hope to preserve, protect, and defend the Constitution of the United States and fundamental freedoms we have been bequeathed as Americans. In moments of doubt, we must always recall the fundamental truism of our yet uncertain existence on this small planet: in the end, God wins.

Let us persist in our resolve that by supporting President Trump, we have chosen to be on the right side of history.

Let us join President Trump in making America great again.

With the help of God, we the deplorables pray we will be able to propel President Trump to victory in this project of killing of the Deep State that we have undertaken together.

PART 1

The Deep State Embraces the #NeverTrump Movement

CHAPTER **1**

The Smoking Gun

This man cannot be president.

—Lisa Page, FBI agent, March 2016

THROUGHOUT 2017, DESPITE NO clear evidence of collusion between Russia and the Trump campaign, the mainstream media continued the negative drumbeat. Obsessed with coverage of FBI Director Comey's firing as obstruction of justice, the mainstream media and Deep State forces glossed over Deputy Attorney General Rod Rosenstein's own conflict of interest in the case. Rosenstein picked the prosecutor to investigate Comey's firing even though Rosenstein himself played a central role in that firing. But by the end of 2017, the Deep State's grip on the coverage took a shocking turn, with proof of anti-Trump forces at work in the FBI.

The turn came with an investigation that Michael Horowitz, the inspector general of the Department of Justice, undertook to determine if preelection bias among top officials in the DOJ caused them to make decisions favorable to Hillary Clinton and prejudicial to Donald Trump.

On or about December 12, 2017, in advance of General Horowitz releasing emails from top DOJ officials to fulfill an oversight request of the House Judiciary Committee, the Department of Justice—without consulting with General Horowitz—turned over 375 text messages exchanged between FBI counterintelligence agent Peter Strzok and FBI attorney Lisa Page.[1] These messages quickly moved to the center of an intensifying argument by Republican members of Congress that members of Special Counsel Robert Mueller's Russia probe were biased against President Trump.

The 375 released text messages opened up a floodgate of information that strongly suggested the FBI and DOJ had conspired to prevent Hillary Clinton from being prosecuted over her email scandal while simultaneously setting up the pretext that Donald Trump's campaign had colluded with Russia to prevent Trump from serving as president should he win the 2016 election.

The Smoking Gun Text Message

In total, General Horowitz obtained some 10,000 text messages exchanged between Strzok and Page over their government-issued cell phones from August 2015 to December 2016. The intensity of the anti-Trump hate sentiment shared by Strzok and Page was perhaps magnified by the extramarital affair the two were enjoying while the text messages were exchanged. Also at that time, both Strzok and Page were working on Mueller's special prosecutor team. Strzok had played a lead role in conducting the FBI investigation into Hillary Clinton's use of a private email server while she was secretary of state.

In August 2015, Page wrote to Strzok, "I just saw my first Bernie Sander [*sic*] bumper sticker. Made me want to key the car." Strzok replied, "He's an idiot like Trump. Figure they cancel each other out." In March 2016, Strzok wondered whether Trump would be a worse president than Senator Ted Cruz. Page answered, "Trump? Yes, I think so." Strzok then added that Trump is "awful" and "an idiot." Strzok called the Republican National Convention in Cleveland "pathetic." In a longer message, Strzok complained, "He [Trump] appears to have no ability to experience reverence which I [*sic*] the foundation for any capacity to admire or serve anything bigger than self to want to learn about anything beyond self, to want to know and deeply honor the people around you." Page wrote back, "He's not ever going to become president, right? Right?" On Election Day, Strzok saw an election map on television that showed Trump winning, which prompted him to express his horror, calling the map "f***ing terrifying."[2]

The smoking gun text message was dated August 15, 2016, with Strzok telling Page, "I want to believe the path you threw out for consideration in Andy's office, that there's no way he [Trump] gets elected—but I'm afraid we can't take that risk. It is like an insurance policy in the likely event you die before you're 40." Page does not appear to have responded. But the reference to "Andy" is to then associate deputy FBI director Andrew McCabe, a controversial figure in the FBI investigation into Secretary of State Hillary Clinton's email server.

What Strzok's message makes clear is that Page and Strzok, in the presence of a high-ranking FBI official, had laid out an "insurance policy" plan to make sure Trump never served his term as president, even if Trump pulled off a miracle to win the election and beat Strzok and Page's clear favorite, Hillary Clinton. Soon it developed that the "insurance policy" involved the Russian collusion evidence the FBI had been quietly accumulating against the Trump campaign. The frightening prospect conveyed by Strzok's text message was that a small group of politically biased FBI officials at the very top of the organization were determined to both make sure Hillary was never indicted or prosecuted and make sure sufficient evidence to impeach Trump was available in the unlikely event that he should be elected president.

Put simply, Strzok's text message from August 15, 2016, would be Exhibit 1 should Strzok, Page, and McCabe ever be indicted for treason for plotting a coup d'état against a legitimately elected president of the United States. What the text message also shows is that the Russian collusion theme was developed briefly during the campaign, but the narrative was not considered particularly important because Obama never made it an issue at that time. But after the election, the Russian collusion story came front and center, the core argument that would be developed in an effort to deny Trump the presidency. Had Hillary been elected president, the nation probably would never have heard anything more about the Russian collusion meme. Hillary did not lose the election because of Russian collusion; Hillary lost the election because she did not pay enough attention to counting Electoral College votes.

As the second-highest-ranking official in counterintelligence, Strzok helped lead the FBI's investigation of Hillary's private email server and approved the bureau's July 2016 investigation into Russian meddling.[3] Electronic records show that Strzok changed a key phrase in the language FBI Director James Comey used on July 5, 2016, in a public statement designed to describe how former secretary of state Hillary Clinton handled classified information. Strzok was responsible for striking language that described Clinton's actions as "grossly negligent"—clearly a crime under national security statutes—and altering it to "extremely careless," a phrase designed to suggest that Clinton bore no criminal responsibility for her actions. Senate Judiciary Committee Chairman Charles Grassley, an Iowa Republican, reacted in anger, writing to the FBI, "Although Director Comey's original version of his statement acknowledged that Secretary Clinton had violated the statute prohibiting gross negligence in the handling of classified information, he nonetheless exonerated her in that early, May 2nd draft statement anyway, arguing that this part of the statute should not be enforced."[4]

Still, in his prepared remarks, Comey managed to fire a shot across Hillary's bow, making it clear that Hillary's handling of classified material had been dangerously close to the language the statute specified as criminal. By doing this, Comey demonstrated that the Deep State was still running the show, even though no one seriously believed Trump had a chance of winning.

In August 2017, when Special Counsel Mueller first learned of the text exchange between Strzok and Page, Strzok was ousted from Mueller's team and reassigned to the FBI's Human Relations Department. On August 16, 2017, ABC News reported that Strzok left Mueller's team investigating Russian collusion, although Mueller continued the cover-up, refusing to explain

even to Congress why Strzok was dismissed.[5] A little more than
a month later, ABC News reported on September 28, 2017, that
Mueller's team lost its second investigator, Lisa Page, who had
been described as recently as June 2017 by *Wired* magazine as
a veteran trial attorney—a key part of Mueller's "investigatory
dream team" who had "deep experience in money laundering and
organized crime cases."[6] Again, Mueller refused to explain even to
Congress why Lisa Page was fired.

The reason for Strzok's and Page's dismissal from Mueller's
special counsel team remained secret until December 2017, when
the DOJ shared with Congress a sample of 375 text messages from
the 10,000 messages Inspector General Horowitz found Strzok
and Page had exchanged between August 2015 and December
2016. Both Special Counsel Mueller and Deputy Attorney General
Rod Rosenstein—the DOJ official, initially an Obama appointee,
to whom Mueller reported after Attorney General Jeff Sessions
recused himself in the Russia collusion investigation—had covered up all information about the Strzok-Page text messages in
order to hide from the public the amount of anti-Trump hatred
there was at the head of the FBI and DOJ during the election and
afterward, leading to Rosenstein's decision to appoint Mueller as
special counsel. Once the American public learned the truth, the
credibility of not only Mueller's special counsel investigation but
also the FBI and the DOJ was seriously tarnished.

Strzok's involvement in the Clinton email investigation was
extensive, with FBI records documenting that Strzok attended
the FBI's interview with Hillary Clinton on July 2, 2016, just
days before then FBI director James Comey read a public statement announcing he was declining to recommend prosecution
of Clinton in connection with her use, as secretary of state, of a
private email server. The FBI interview with Clinton was taken
without Clinton being placed under oath and without a verbatim
transcript being made. Strzok appears to have been involved in
a series of FBI decisions that granted immunity to key Clinton

aides involved with the private email server controversy, including Clinton's longtime legal confidant Cheryl Mills. In his counter-intelligence position, Strzok also enjoyed liaison with various agencies in the intelligence community, including the CIA, then led by director John Brennan, a longtime supporter of and advisor to President Barack Obama.[7]

FBI Deputy Director Andrew McCabe

Campaign finance records show that a political action committee tied to Virginia governor Terry McAuliffe, an influential Democrat political operative with financial ties to Bill and Hillary Clinton, donated $467,500 to Jill McCabe in 2015 to assist her in her race for a Virginia state senate seat. Campaign finance records further reveal that the Virginia Democratic Party, over which Governor McAuliffe exerted considerable control, donated an additional $207,788 of support to McCabe's campaign in the form of mailers.

This adds up to $675,000 donated by McAuliffe and the Democratic Party in Virginia to McCabe's wife while he was associate deputy director of the FBI and one of a small group at the head of the FBI during the 2016 presidential campaign responsible for investigating Hillary's email server. The 2015 Virginia state senate race was Jill McCabe's first run for office, and her campaign spent $1.8 million in the losing effort.[8] On October 23, 2016, McCabe wrote an email to the press indicating the Clinton email server investigation had assumed "special status" and was being moved to the control of a small group of high-ranking people at the FBI headquarters in Washington, which included McCabe.[9] On January 29, 2016, FBI Director James Comey appointed McCabe as deputy director of the FBI.

When President Trump fired Director James Comey on May 9, 2017, McCabe, then the deputy director, became the acting director of the FBI. Among the issues DOJ Inspector General Horowitz is investigating is whether McCabe should have recused himself from participating in the FBI's Russia investigation, given the conflicts of interest crated by his wife's funding from Terry McAuliffe and the Democratic Party in Virginia.[10]

Bruce and Nellie Ohr

The Mueller investigation was rocked once again in early December, when the DOJ announced a very senior official, Bruce Ohr, had been demoted. Until being demoted, Ohr held two titles at DOJ: associate deputy attorney general, a position that put him four doors down on the fourth floor of "Main Justice" from his boss, Deputy Attorney General Rod Rosenstein, and a second position as director of the Organized Crime Drug Enforcement Task Force, a program described by DOJ as "the centerpiece of the attorney's general's drug strategy."[11]

Ohr was demoted after evidence collected by the House Permanent Select Committee on Intelligence, chaired by Representative Devin Nunes, a Republican from California, revealed that Ohr had met during the 2016 presidential campaign with Christopher Steele, the British intelligence agent at the center of the controversy surrounding an opposition research dossier prepared against candidate Donald Trump. Additionally, House Intelligence Committee investigators have determined that Ohr met shortly after the election with Glenn Simpson, the founder of Fusion GPS, the opposition research firm that hired Steele to complete the dossier with funds supplied by Hillary Clinton's campaign and the Democratic National Committee.[12] The payments to Fusion GPS from the Clinton campaign and the DNC were made indirectly, laundered as legal payments to the Seattle-based law firm Perkins Coie, a longtime advisor to Democratic Party politicians, including President Barack Obama.

As will be more completely discussed in chapter 7, the FBI embraced the Fusion GPS dossier despite a body of evidence suggesting its research into the Trump campaign's possible collusion with Russia was flawed by the same anti-Trump bias that appears to have permeated the top echelons of the FBI and the DOJ, casting doubts on the integrity of Mueller's special counsel investigation. From published reports, Strzok, then acting in his counterintelligence position, was the FBI official who first took possession in of the Fusion GPS Russia dossier, possibly as early as five months before the November 2016 election.

According to Fox News senior judicial analyst Judge Andrew Napolitano, the FBI appears to have offered the former British spy Christopher Steele $50,000 if he could corroborate the Fusion GPS findings.[13] Appearing before the House Intelligence Committee on December 13, 2017, Deputy Director Rosenstein refused to answer directly as to whether the FBI used the Fusion GPS Russia dossier as the basis to obtain a warrant from the US Foreign Intelligence Surveillance Court under the Foreign Intelligence Surveillance Act (FISA) to conduct electronic surveillance on members of Donald Trump's 2016 campaign.[14] If the Fusion GPS Russia dossier proves to have included false information derogatory to Trump, the FBI's use of the document runs the risk of compromising Mueller's Russia investigation, especially if the FBI used the Fusion GPS dossier as the basis for obtaining court-authorized approval to conduct electronic surveillance on members of the Trump campaign.

Bruce Ohr was demoted not only because he refused to disclose his meeting with Steele and Simpson over the Fusion GPS dossier to the FBI but also because he failed to disclose that his wife, Nellie Ohr, was hired by Fusion GPS to work on the Russia dossier. It turns out that Fusion GPS put Nellie on the payroll because of her obvious close ties to the FBI and because she is a Russian speaker with ties to the CIA who holds advanced academic degrees in Russian literature and history.

Federal Communications Commission records also document that Nellie Ohr obtained an amateur ham radio license on May 23, 2016, after she was hired by Fusion GPS.[15] Those investigating Nellie Ohr's role in the controversy suggest she might have done so to communicate "outside the normal risk of communication intercepts" with Christopher Steele, the British intelligence agent responsible for producing the Fusion GPS opposition research dossier on Donald Trump and/or with various sources in Russia that Steele was utilizing to develop the opposition research he planned to use to sink the Trump campaign.[16] Glenn Simpson, a cofounder of Fusion GPS, hired Nellie Ohr the month before, in April 2016, to work as a subcontractor for Russian contacts, including those purporting to have highly inflammatory but unsubstantiated allegations believed to be detrimental to Trump's campaign if made public.[17]

Nellie Ohr speaks fluent Russian and holds a BA in Russian history and literature from Harvard and a PhD in Russian history from Stanford; she has been a Russia scholar at the Wilson Center and taught at Vassar College.[18] Nellie and Bruce Ohr are both listed as working in a June 2010 National Institute of Justice Expert Working Group on International Organized Crime, with Bruce Ohr working as the chief of the Organized Crime and Racketeering Section, Criminal Division, US Department of Justice, and Nellie Ohr identified as a researcher with the CIA's Open Source Works in Washington.[19]

The Wilson Center identifies Ohr as an assistant professor at Vassar College, who from August 1, 1997, through October 1, 1997, had a short-term grant with the Kennan Institute to study "collective farmers of Russia's Western Region after collectivization and under German occupation."[20] A résumé for Nellie Ohr posted on the internet shows she was a former review editor for H-Russia, a member of H-Net Humanities and Social Sciences Online.[21] Listed as her major published work to date was a research paper titled "After Collectivization: Social Capital and Local Politics in Rural Western Russia, 1933–1937," an article that was translated into Russian.

Nellie Ohr's maiden name is Hauke; she is the daughter of Dr. Kathleen Armstrong Hauke, a resident of Arlington, Virginia, who was a writer known for popularizing the works of African American journalist Ted Poston, who traveled to the Soviet Union with poet Langston Hughes in 1932.[22] A book titled *Adventures in Russian Historical Research* documents that Ohr was in Moscow doing research, supposedly for her doctoral dissertation, at the Lenin Library in Moscow during 1989.[23]

Andrew Weissmann and Sally Yates

An email obtained by Judicial Watch through a Freedom of Information Act (FOIA) request shows that on the night of January 30, 2017, former DOJ prosecutor Andrew Weissmann sent an email to former acting attorney general Sally Yates with the subject line, "I am so proud of you." In the three-sentence body of the email, Weissmann said, "And in awe. Thank you so much. All my deepest respects."[24]

The background of the memo was that President Trump had just fired Yates after an escalating crisis in which Yates, who had served as deputy attorney general under President Obama, had refused to carry out President Trump's executive order that the political left was interpreting to be a travel ban against Muslims.[25] Tom Fitton of Judicial Watch said the email was "an astonishing and disturbing find." Weissmann had just taken a leave with the DOJ to serve as a top prosecutor on Mueller's special counsel team. Since 2015, Weissmann had headed DOJ's criminal fraud division. "Andrew Weissmann, a key prosecutor on Robert Mueller's team, praised Obama DOJ holdover Sally Yates after she lawlessly thwarted President Trump," Fitton said. "How much more evidence do we need that the Mueller operation has been irredeemably compromised by anti-Trump partisans?"[26]

As a prosecutor, Weissmann has a reputation for being fast and loose with the rules in his zeal to obtain convictions. Sidney Powell—a former US attorney whose 2014 book *Licensed to Lie: Exposing Corruption in the Department of Justice* is a shocking exposé of prosecutorial impropriety that she maintains runs rampant today among Department of Justice prosecutors—warns that Andrew Weissmann, a federal prosecutor who is now part of Mueller's team, is capable of extorting guilty pleas. Powell points to the example of former Arthur Anderson partner David Duncan, who withdrew his guilty plea in the Enron case after Weissmann extorted him to testify for the government to obtain the wrongful conviction of Arthur Anderson. Noting that Weissmann was the "driving force" behind the indictment of Arthur Anderson in the Enron case, Weissmann used the "special tactics" he developed prosecuting organized criminals, convinced that even if some of his special tactics went outside the bounds, the ends justified the means when prosecuting serious bad guys. Later in the book, Powell points out that Weissmann forced Duncan into a guilty plea by misrepresenting Duncan's innocent conduct in the case as "criminal."[27]

CHAPTER 2

A Shattering Defeat and the Left's Paradise Lost

The election of Donald Trump to the
Presidency is nothing less than a tragedy.

—David Remnick, *The New Yorker*

A T 11:05 A.M. ET ON June 16, 2015, when Donald and Mela-nia Trump descended from the mezzanine of Trump Tower in New York City to announce Donald Trump's candidacy for president, US politics entered a revolutionary era. Almost imme-diately, the mainstream media began characterizing Trump's candidacy as a joke, predicting his demise. Trump would never win in the primaries, most insisted. Then, when Trump surged in the primaries, the mainstream media changed the theme, pre-dicting Trump would never get enough delegates for a first ballot win at the Republican national nominating convention in Cleve-land. In the end, Trump's victory in the primaries was decisive, winning 41 primaries and getting some 500 delegates more than the 1,237 he needed to secure the GOP presidential nomination on the first ballot.

Even as the nation prepared to vote on November 8, 2016, com-mentators on cable television remained unanimous in their opin-ions that Trump was losing badly in the polls and that Hillary was certain to win the presidency. Democrats began the 2016 presi-dential campaign with "a mortal lock" on 246 of the 270 electoral votes needed to win.[1] Pundit after pundit insisted that Trump would lose some of the largest states with the greatest num-ber of electoral votes, including both New York and California. According to the experts, he had "no electoral path" available to win enough of the remaining states to get the 270 electoral votes needed for victory.

Yet at 2:45 a.m. ET, after the voting was done, television net-works announced to a stunned nation that Pennsylvania's 20 electoral votes had gone to Donald Trump, making him the president-elect of the United States. Donald Trump had defied all odds, winning a surreal victory that sent the Deep State into an immediate panic.

A leaked video showed an elated Clinton family prematurely celebrating victory on election night based on early results indicating that Hillary would be elected president, just as predicted. The video shows Chelsea running into her mother's open arms, embracing a smiling Hillary, while Bill Clinton claps his hands and jumps up and down like an excited schoolboy.[2] Too bad for the Clintons the elation did not last long.

In R. Emmett Tyrrell's blog on *The American Spectator* website, sources reported that Hillary flew into a rage after it was clear she had lost. According to Secret Service officers, Hillary pounded the furniture and screamed obscenities—throwing objects at staff in an uncontrollable fury.

The Glass Ceiling

As the *New York Post* noted in reporting Clinton's historic defeat, Hillary had chosen every detail of her election night so as to mark her moment in history—from the glass ceiling at Manhattan's Javits Center, where hundreds of supporters were gathered to hear her victory speech, to the top-floor suite the Clintons had reserved at the Peninsula Hotel, located at 5th Avenue and 55th Street. Hillary had selected that hotel "so she could personally see Trump Tower, home to the foe she was set to crush."

"Hillary's communications team decamped to the Javits Center in the Hell's Kitchen section of Manhattan, where preparations for her victory party were being made," the *New York Post* noted. "The venue, which would fill with Hillary aides, donors, friends and well-wishers over the course of the day, was chosen in large part because of its distinctive feature: a glass ceiling. If everything went as planned, it would be the glass ceiling of the presidency that lay shattered under Hillary by the end of the night."[3]

At 2:00 a.m. ET, Hillary's campaign chairman, John Podesta, appeared at the podium in the Javits Center to say, "Well, folks, I know you have been here a long time, and it's been a long night and a long campaign. But I can say, we can wait a little longer, can't we? They are still counting votes, and every vote should count. Several states are too close to call, so we're not going to have anything more to say tonight." That was it, no concession. "So listen, listen to me," Podesta continued, "everybody should head home. We should get some sleep."

But President Obama phoned Hillary at the Peninsula to impress upon her the inevitable. The White House had concluded that the electoral map as reported by the television coverage was correct. Despite all the predictions, including nearly unanimous polling data that predicted Hillary would win easily, she had lost. Obama urged Hillary to telephone Trump and concede.

Finally, Hillary reluctantly agreed to speak with Trump by telephone. In a short call, Hillary conceded. "Congratulations, Donald," she said. "I'll be supportive of the country's success, and that means your success as president."[4]

Hillary's Defeat: "An American Tragedy"

The next day, David Remnick, the author of a 2010 book titled *The Bridge: The Life and Rise of Barack Obama*, delivered the political left's verdict on Trump's unanticipated victory in the *New Yorker*. "The election of Donald Trump to the Presidency is nothing less than a tragedy for the American republic, a tragedy for the Constitution, and a triumph for the forces, at home and abroad, of nativism, authoritarianism, misogyny, and racism," Remnick wrote. "Trump's shocking victory, his ascension to the Presidency, is a sickening event in the history of the United States and liberal democracy." Already, Remnick was lamenting the passing out of office of Barack Obama. "On January 20, 2017, we will bid farewell to the first African-American President—a man of integrity, dignity, and generous spirit—and witness the inauguration of a

con who did little to spurn endorsement by forces of xenopho-
bia and white supremacy," he insisted. "It is impossible to react
to this moment with anything less than revulsion and profound
anxiety."[5]

This was the first salvo suggesting that the Hillary camp was
not about to accept defeat so easily. Clearly the political left
could not allow American voters to elect to the presidency a
person David Remnick and like-minded ideologues in the New
York, Washington, and Los Angeles media elite had designated
as not qualified to be president. Donald Trump was so politically
incorrect, the elite felt certain that somehow, he would have to be
barred from taking the oath of office.

The next day, on November 9, 2016, Hillary gave a formal
concession speech, saying, "Last night, I congratulated Donald
Trump and offered to work with him on behalf of our country.
I hope that he will be a successful president for all people."[6] The
emphasis on "all people" appeared to be a subtle reference to
Hillary's repeated charges that Trump's campaign was a divisive
one, designed to appeal only to the reactionary impulses of white
supremacists seeking to roll back the "social justice" achieve-
ments of the Obama administration.

Within 24 hours of her formal concession speech, an angry
and aggrieved Hillary refused to take responsibility for her loss
to Trump, pointing her finger instead at Russia, resentful that
Obama had not done more to make the case that Vladimir Putin
had targeted her in a determined effort to throw the election to
Trump.[7]

The Russian Collusion Meme Emerges

During the campaign, the Deep State had begun planting the
seeds of a key strategy it would use to declare Trump's victory
illegitimate so as to bar him from the White House. "American
intelligence agencies have told the White House they now have
'high confidence' that the Russian government was behind the

theft of emails and documents from the Democratic National Committee, according to federal officials who have been briefed on the evidence," the *New York Times* reported on July 26, 2016.[8]

This followed an article published by the *Times* on June 14, 2016, claiming, "Two groups of Russian hackers, working for competing government intelligence agencies, penetrated computer systems of the Democratic National Committee and gained access to emails, chats and a trove of opposition research against Donald J. Trump according to the party and a cybersecurity firm."[9] The newspaper further reported that the DNC had called in Crowd-Strike, a private security firm, which identified "Cozy Bear" and "Fancy Bear" as the two Russian intelligence agencies culpable for the hacking, although the article failed to document precisely how CrowdStrike determined the hack was from Russian intelligence agencies. The *New York Times* assured readers that, again, unnamed "investigators" had attributed the hacks to a person who called himself "Guccifer 2.0," identified as an agent of the GRU, Russia's military intelligence service. The *Times* reporting quickly became the accepted version of events, such that anyone doubting that the Russians had hacked the DNC would be tagged as advancing a "conspiracy theory."

Then on July 27, 2016, at a press conference in Miami, Florida, Trump commented, "Russia, if you are listening, I hope you are able to find the 30,000 emails that are missing."[10] This was in reference to the 30,000 State Department emails Hillary destroyed after deciding that they were "personal . . . and within the scope of my personal privacy," despite knowing they were subject to preservation orders under a congressional subpoena.[11] Trump concluded the press conference by stressing that he would treat Vladimir "firmly, but there's nothing I can think of that I'd rather do than have Russia friendly as opposed to the way they are right now, so that we can go and knock out ISIS together."

This was all Hillary campaign operatives and the mainstream media needed to charge that Trump had been the driving force behind the theft of DNC emails, in collusion with Russia to make sure Hillary lost the election. For damage control, the Trump campaign was forced to "walk back" Trump's statement, claiming that all Trump meant was that if Russia had the 30,000 emails Hillary had destroyed, they should be turned over to the FBI.

Despite the lack of verifiable proof, Hillary and the mainstream media made the Russia narrative during the campaign one that suggested Trump had worked with Russia to win the election by hacking the DNC. According to the developing "Russian collusion" meme, Trump's devious plan was to induce Russia to release to DC Leaks and WikiLeaks the purloined Democratic emails and other confidential Clinton documents stolen by Guccifer 2.0 and/or Russian intelligence agencies identified only as "Cozy Bear" and "Fancy Bear."

During the first presidential debate at Hofstra University in Hempstead, New York, Hillary returned to the Russia meme. "There's no doubt now that Russia has used cyberattacks against all kinds of organizations in our country, and I am deeply concerned about this," Hillary said. "I know Donald's very praiseworthy of Vladimir Putin, but Putin is playing a really tough long game here." Then a few minutes later, she added, "I was so shocked when Donald publicly invited Putin to hack into Americans. That is just unacceptable."

Notice that Trump's initial statement did not invite Russia to hack the DNC computers. Trump was making an offhand quip, suggesting that if the *New York Times's* unnamed intelligence sources were right and Russia was responsible for hacking the DNC computers, then maybe Russia had possession of the 30,000 emails Hillary had destroyed. The point that a Deep State narrative need not be true is important. Even distorted, as Hillary distorted Trump's offhand press conference comment, a meme can take hold if it is repeated enough times without question or criticism. Over a relatively short time, the distorted version becomes the official version of what Trump said and what he meant. From this point on, the Deep State's assertion that Trump was in collusion with Russia to steal the election from Hillary was firmly planted in the mainstream media narrative of campaign events.

The Deep State Resolves to Deny Trump the White House

On January 6, 2016, a partially declassified intelligence community assessment commissioned by President Obama and issued by the office of the director of national intelligence (DNI) concluded that Russia had interfered with the US presidential election in a bid to help Trump.

"We assess Russian President Vladimir Putin ordered an influence campaign in 2016 aimed at the US presidential election. Russia's goals were to undermine public faith in the US democratic process, denigrate Secretary Clinton, and harm her electability and potential presidency," the DNI report said. "We further assess Putin and the Russian Government developed a clear preference for President-elect Trump. We have high confidence in these judgments," the report continued. The report concluded that Putin "most likely wanted to discredit Secretary Clinton because he has publicly blamed her since 2011 for inciting mass protests against his regime in late 2011 and early 2012 and because he holds a grudge for comments he almost certainly saw as disparaging him."[12]

The DNI report stressed that the CIA, FBI, and National Security Agency (NSA) all agreed with this judgment. With this report, the Deep State positioned the "Russian collusion" meme as its first-choice strategy for blocking Donald Trump from becoming president. In contrast, by December 13, 2000, Al Gore had abandoned his presidential bid, accepting the decision of the Supreme Court as a campaign-ending decision; in December 2016, the DNI intelligence report gave Democrats new hope that Hilary Clinton may yet be inaugurated as president—if Trump's collusion with Russia could be proven. With the publication of this intelligence community assessment, the Deep State game to deny Donald J. Trump the presidency was on in earnest. As former Director of National Intelligence James Clapper said on *Meet the Press* in March 2017, "We did not include any evidence in our report, and I say, 'our,' that's NSA, FBI and CIA, with my office, the Director of National Intelligence, that had anything, that had any reflection of collusion between members of the Trump campaign and the Russians. There was no evidence of that included in our report."

Paradise Lost

Hillary not only lost the opportunity to shatter the glass ceiling on Election Night 2016; her supporters also lost the opportunity to create a far-left utopia that they felt was certainly within their grasp. With Hillary as president, Obama could look forward to a continuation of his eight-year Saul Alinsky–like effort to fundamentally transform the United States into a socialist nation that warmly embraced radical Islamic extremists, including the Muslim Brotherhood.

With the Democrats thrown into disarray by Hillary's defeat, the party resolved to move further to the left, determined to pursue a radical hard-left agenda consistent with the Deep State's determination that Donald Trump must never be permitted to govern.

After eight years in office, Barack Obama had set the stage for a Hillary Clinton presidency that would once and for all time recast the American charter with new legislation and Supreme Court decisions that would transform what Obama had achieved into a final rewriting of the American covenant. Where our Founding Fathers desired to limit government power to protect and preserve individual liberties, the Democrats under Obama and Hillary sought to establish a Marxist-leaning social welfare state consistent with globalist one-world-government ambitions.

Hillary Clinton's speeches to Goldman Sachs left no doubt that her political philosophy called for statist control over an international bank–driven finance system supporting the development of international business dominating a global economy.

Hillary's America

Imagine how different the United States would have been had Hillary won the presidential election, defeating Donald Trump in 2016. Her ambitions to extend Obama's social welfare state and identity politics to a new level was clear, given her many campaign pronouncements and the public policy statements published on her campaign website.

Hillary and her supporters felt that with her victory, the achievement of a totalitarian far-left utopia was within their reach. In short, if Hillary had won, the hard-left Alinsky acolytes taking over the Democratic Party would have had the chance to eliminate from the United States all those Hillary defined as "irredeemable deplorables"—that is, people she saw as "racist, sexist, homophobic, xenophobic, [and] Islamaphobic" Trump supporters.

In her postelection book, *What Happened*, Hillary speculated that her presidency "would have been transformative" by implementing higher minimum wages, expanding social welfare programs, and increasing government intervention into our economic and social lives by a host of new regulations imposed by an ever-expanding corps of unelected bureaucrats.

The Deep State's Plan to Recover Paradise Lost

The sense of frustration felt by the left with Hillary Clinton's demise was so enormous as to be almost immeasurable. The November 2016 edition of the leftist publication the *Nation* appeared with a black cover, on which were printed the following words, with the first appearing in small print in gray, then proceeding to large print in white: "Mourn, Resist, Organize, Onward."

"And so many of our hopes—for free public college, a livable minimum wage, expanded Social Security, a path to universal health care, paid family leave, an end to private prisons, the abolition of the death penalty—now lie shattered, along with the prospect of an administration that, whatever its limitations, had been shown to be open to pressure from the left," wrote D. D. Guttenplan, an at-large editor for the publication. "Which means we have to apply even greater pressure from the left: to march in greater numbers, to shout out louder against injustice, and to summon and be prepared to sustain everyday massive nonviolent civil disobedience on a scale not seen in this country for decades."[13]

To be so close, with what appeared to be a certain win for Hillary Clinton, and yet to lose was devastating for Hillary's most committed supporters. Hillary Democrats were determined to see if the mounting resistance could prevent Trump from being inaugurated. If the resistance movement failed there, the focus would shift to identifying strategies that could lead to his impeachment and removal from office. At a minimum, Democratic Party resistance could transform into an obstruction movement that would prevent Donald Trump from enacting into legislation the public policy objectives he had articulated while running for president. An aggressive Democratic Party resist-and-obstruct movement, even if unsuccessful, could impair the effectiveness of the Trump presidency.

But for these dark, resentful, but determined Democratic ambitions to succeed, the Democrats knew they could count on the willing and enthusiastic cooperation of the Deep State.

CHAPTER 3

The Deep State Targets Trump

So I don't think it's Trump versus Obama;
I think it's really the Deep State versus the
president, the duly elected president.

—Representative Thomas Massie
(Republican, Kentucky),
February 2017

A S EVIDENCE OF THE Deep State's antipathy toward Trump, one needs to look no further than at the illegal unmasking of US citizens that took place numerous times during the Trump campaign. This unmasking is a certain breach of the democratic process and shows the Deep State was out to get Trump—and would violate the law to do so. The concept of "deep politics" entered the national dialogue in a serious manner when the American public realized that there were dark forces at work behind shocking events. In 1976, the Church Committee concluded that the Warren Commission covered up the role organized crime had played working with the CIA to assassinate President John Fitzgerald Kennedy. Ever since Watergate, the American public have come to expect that what we observe in the "overt politics" reported by the mainstream media has nothing to do with the "deep politics," in which hidden forces predominate. The truth of the American Republic in the new millennium is that we have become accustomed to mobsters working with government intelligence agency drug dealers, financed by Wall Street and banks that are "too big to fail." In the background are K-Street lobbyists in Washington ready to shape public policy and congressional legislation in favor of international corporations and the global elite who pay their hefty lobbying fees.

"The term [Deep State] was actually coined in Turkey and is said to be a system composed of high-level elements within the intelligence services, military, security, judiciary, and organized crime," wrote retired congressional staff budget analyst Mike Lofgren in his 2016 book *The Deep State: The Fall of the Constitution and the Rise of a Shadow Government*.[1] Lofgren has defined traditional

Washington partisan politics as "the tip of the iceberg that a pub
lic watching C-SPAN sees daily and which is theoretically control-
lable via elections." But the Deep State "operates according to its
own compass regardless of who is formally in power."[2] This chapter explores three short vignettes from US history that demonstrate why President Trump must take seriously the threat to his
presidency and his life represented by a Deep State that remains
determined to remove him from office.

Unable to accept that Donald Trump might win the 2016
elections, the NSA in cooperation with CIA Director John
Brennan—Barack Obama's handler in the CIA since Obama
emerged in national politics by winning a Senate seat in Illinois
in 2006—began placing Trump and his aides under extensive electronic surveillance in an attempt to derail Trump's candidacy.
As WikiLeaks prepared to publish the emails of top Democratic
National Committee (DNC) officials, including Hillary Clinton's campaign chairman, John Podesta, leaked from within the
DNC, Brennan championed the "Russian collusion" narrative,
seeking to delegitimize the Trump campaign. After the election,
the CIA conspired with Democrats in Congress and the mainstream media to have Robert Mueller appointed as special counsel. Mueller was widely known in Washington as a former FBI
director and a partisan Deep State operative with close ties to
FBI Director James Comey. As special counselor, Mueller had one
mission—namely, to develop the information needed to accuse
Trump of rigging the election with Russia's assistance. The plan
called for Democrats in Congress to beat the mainstream media
drum until Trump resigned or stepped aside for Vice President
Mike Pence.

Should the Deep State fail to remove Trump from office
through impeachment or a charge under the 25th Amendment that he is mentally incompetent, "executive action"—a
CIA plan to assassinate Trump—is the Deep State's last resort.[3]

The point is, unless Trump can be made to abandon his "America First" agenda, the globalists in the Deep State have already decided that Trump must be removed from the presidency—one way or the other.

The Military-Industrial Complex

The first vignette involves a warning that President Dwight D. Eisenhower issued to America upon leaving the White House after eight years as president. On January 17, 1961, President Eisenhower delivered his farewell speech to the nation in a televised address broadcast from the Oval Office. In that speech, Eisenhower sounded an alarm to future generations of Americans. "In the councils of government, we must guard against the acquisition of unwarranted influence, whether sought or unsought, by the military-industrial complex," Eisenhower warned. "The potential for the disastrous rise of misplaced power exists and will persist." He continued with a sentiment that is less frequently repeated. "We must never let the weight of this combination endanger our liberties or democratic processes," he stressed. "We should take nothing for granted. Only an alert and knowledgeable citizenry can compel the proper meshing of the huge industrial and military machinery of defense with our peaceful methods and goals, so that security and liberty may prosper together."[4]

The Shadow Government

CIA whistleblower Kevin Shipp, a decorated CIA intelligence officer, has identified the CIA as the "central node" of the shadow government that controls all of the other 16 intelligence agencies, despite the existence of the director of national intelligence. According to Shipp, the Deep State is composed of the military-industrial complex and its lobbyists, intelligence contractors, defense contractors, Wall Street (through offshore accounts), the Federal Reserve, the International Monetary Fund and the

World Bank, the US Treasury Department, foreign lobbyists, and central banks. To this list, we can reinsert Congress—the group President Eisenhower knew votes to fund and protect the Deep State's massive, largely unchecked, clandestine operations. Shipp claims the CIA "controls defense and intelligence contractors, can manipulate the president and presidential decisions, has the power to start wars, torture, initiate coups, and commit false flag attacks."[5]

Peter Dale Scott has come to view the Kennedy assassination, Watergate, the 1980 October Surprise involving the release of the US embassy hostages in the Iran–Contra affair, and 9/11 as Deep State events that "repeatedly have involved lawbreaking and/or violence, have been mysterious to begin with, and whose mystery has been compounded by systematic falsifications in media and internal government records." Scott has come to see these incidents as "flowing in part from the sociodynamic processes of violent power itself, power associated with and deployed in the service of the global expansion of American military might." Focusing on what he has called the "American War Machine," Scott has advanced the understanding of the extent to which Eisenhower's military-industrial complex has led to the operation of an extra-Constitutional Deep State willing to use the black political arts of false-flag attacks, funding of mainstream media propaganda, and even assassination of heads of state to dominate US politics by controlling both political parties.[6]

Obama Administration Illegally Unmasks and Leaks

The volume of mainstream media stories attributed to anonymous sources that were published during the 2016 presidential caused Senator Charles Grassley (Republican, Iowa), the chairman of the Senate Judiciary Committee, and Representative Devin Nunes (Republican, California), the chairman of the House Permanent Select Committee on Intelligence, to become suspicious. Where did the Democrats get their information that Trump officials had conspired or otherwise colluded with Russia? Or even more specifically, unless the Obama administration had unmasked Trump campaign officials captured in NSA surveillance of foreign nationals, how did it begin to suspect that Trump officials were actively conspiring with Russian officials? "Unmasking" involves identifying the US citizens captured in FISA-authorized electronic surveillance of foreign nationals—a process that invites abuse when government officials decide to make the unmasked US citizens the targets of future surveillance. In other words, Obama officials appear to have done just this to get the dirt they needed on Trump officials to construct the Russian collusion narrative. Then, once in possession of the unmasked names, highly placed officials within the Obama administration appear to have committed a second crime by leaking to the press the highly classified information obtained on Trump campaign officials through the NSA Foreign Intelligence Surveillance Court–ordered electronic surveillance.

Investigating the issue, Grassley and Nunes became convinced that the FBI and NSA went one step further, deciding to place foreign nationals believed to be in touch with Trump campaign officials under electronic surveillance, with the intent of capturing Trump campaign officials in communication with the targeted foreign nationals. Even if the FBI or the DOJ were not interested in investigating the foreign nationals, the Obama administration appears to have instructed the NSA to find a way to conduct surveillance on the foreign nationals because the Obama administration wanted to capture Trump campaign officials in conversations with Russian nationals or with foreign operatives that were working with Russian nationals.

Suspicion that unmasking had occurred quickly centered on Obama's national security advisor, Susan Rice; US ambassador to the United Nations, Samantha Power; and CIA director

John Brennan. The question was this: Had President Obama instructed or otherwise allowed Rice, Power, and Brennan to "unmask" Trump campaign officials captured in NSA surveillance of foreign targets in order to develop information that Trump campaign officials were conspiring or otherwise colluding with Russian officials to rig the presidential election?

It appears that once NSA electronic surveillance had captured intelligence appearing to link Trump campaign officials to Russian nationals, the Obama administration next illegally leaked that information to friendly reporters in the mainstream media. This would account for the number of reports accusing Trump campaign officials of colluding with the Russians that the mainstream media attributed to unnamed individuals "close to the investigation." Within the White House, suspicion extended to former deputy national security adviser Ben Rhodes as a lead culprit in leaking to the press the "evidence" of Russian collusion found after Rice, Power, and Brennan unmasked Trump campaign officials captured in NSA electronic surveillance of foreign nationals.[7]

On September 19, 2017, CNN reported that Rice admitted to House Intelligence Committee members that she had unmasked the identities of senior Trump officials to understand why the crown prince of the United Arab Emirates, Mohammed bin Zayed Al-Nahyan, was in New York in 2016.[8] Months earlier, on April 5, 2017, President Trump told reporters that Rice may have committed a crime by seeking to learn the identities of Trump associates swept up in surveillance of foreign officials by US spy agencies. "I think the Susan Rice thing is a massive story," Trump told reporters in the Oval Office. "It's a bigger story than you know. The Russia story is a total hoax. There has been absolutely nothing coming out of that. What's happened is terrible. I've never seen people so indignant, including many Democrats who are friends of mine."[9]

Rice attempted to explain that she asked for the unmasking because Zayed had scheduled a trip to the United States without notifying the Obama administration about travel plans. However, it's more likely that Rice was suspicious that General Mike Flynn, Jared Kushner, and Steve Bannon had discussed opening a back channel to Russia in their three-hour discussion that focused on Iran, Yemen, and the Middle East peace process.

Representative Nunes, in a letter to Director of National Intelligence Dan Coates in July 2017, made clear his concern that all Obama administration leaks of classified information would be vigorously prosecuted. Nunes also alleged in the letter that "Obama-era officials sought the identities of Trump transition officials within intelligence reports." Nunes's concern was that the Obama administration, since before the November 2016 election, had actively conspired to build the "Russian collusion" case against Trump through a process of unmasking intelligence reports and leaking the contents to partisan, Clinton-supporting reporters in the mainstream media.

These suspicions had a basis in fact, given the record of the Obama Department of Justice under both Eric Holder and Loretta Lynch seeking to prosecute and convict political opponents in the press by orchestrating a campaign to leak secret grand jury information to reporters. This practice demanded the Obama administration FBI's active complicity in leaking secret grand jury administration under both FBI directors Robert Mueller and James Comey.

Mueller Illegally Leaks Unmasked Political Intel

That the mainstream media built the case that Trump had colluded with Russia on a mountain of leaks is clear by examining any of a large number of stories that were informed only by anonymous sources and unnamed insiders. On May 27, 2017, for instance, the *New York Times* published an article titled, "Top Russian

Officials Discussed How to Influence Trump Aides Last Summer." The first paragraph of the article read as follows: "American spies collected information last summer revealing that senior Russian intelligence and political officials were discussing how to exert influence over Donald J. Trump through his advisors, according to three current and former American officials familiar with the investigation." None of these sources were named or otherwise identified in the article.[10]

Still, *New York Times* reporters did not hesitate to write that the unnamed Russians focused on Paul Manafort, identified as "Trump campaign chairman at the time," and General Michael Flynn, identified as "a retired general who was advising Mr. Trump." The article insinuated in print that both Manafort and Flynn "had indirect ties to Russian officials, who appeared confident that each could help shape Mr. Trump's opinions on Russia." So in summary, the *Times* article claimed as sources "three current and former American officials familiar with the investigation"—all unnamed—who said unnamed Russian officials who felt they could influence Trump were involved in undocumented conversations with Manafort and Flynn. Finally, the *New York Times* referenced that "intelligence was among the clues," which included information "about direct communications between Mr. Trump's advisors and American officials—that American officials received last year as they began investigating Russian attempts to disrupt the election and whether any of Mr. Trump's associates were assisting Moscow in the effort."[11]

These examples clearly suggest that Obama administration officials had leaked to the *New York Times* information obtained illegally by "unmasking" Trump campaign officials so as to obtain conversations and or emails with them that the NSA obtained through electronic surveillance of foreign nationals. No wonder Grassley and Nunes were suspicious.

Perhaps Mueller's two most blatant leaks were evident first in a *New York Times* story published on September 18, 2017, titled "With a Picked Lock and a Threatened Indictment, Mueller's Inquiry Sets a Tone." In the article, reporters Sharon LaFraniere, Matt Apuzzo, and Adam Goldman made public that Mueller intended to follow his predawn gestapo-like raid into Manafort's Alexandria, Virginia, apartment home with an indictment, according to information the newspaper reported learning from typically anonymous sources identified only as "two people close to the investigation."[12]

Then on Friday, October 27, 2017, Mueller obtained his first indictments in the Russia collusion case from a Washington, DC, grand jury. Yet instead of making the charges public, Mueller had the grand jury seal the indictments until the following Monday, allowing the special counselor's office to leak the news to CNN. This gave Mueller the weekend, including the Sunday morning news programs, to allow Clinton operatives to build the case on television that Manafort, Flynn, and whoever else Mueller had indicted were guilty as charged. Through the weekend, the uncertainty among Trump supporters was heightened by their inability to identify exactly which suspects Mueller had indicted.

Mueller should be forced to explain why he should be allowed to continue his investigation when a pattern of illegal unmasking and illegal leaking of classified information reaches beyond him to include the highest levels of the Obama administration. Proof abounded that Mueller's Russia probe was riddled with systematic government impropriety that would not only justify his firing and disqualify his Russian collusion investigation from being allowed to continue but also demand a criminal investigation of Mueller himself and of the Obama administration officials involved in the illegal unmasking and illegal leaking.

The question is whether Donald Trump is capable, with the support of US patriots, of defeating the Deep State, or whether the Deep State has advanced to the point where it will crush the last vestiges of the Tea Party movement by removing Donald Trump from office. The Deep State will not care if Trump is impeached, declared mentally incompetent, or—as a final resort—assassinated, as long as he is removed from office before the completion of his first term.

CHAPTER 4

The Strategy to Block Trump's Inauguration Fails

Our source is not a state party.

—Julian Assange on the source of the email leaks,
December 2016

WHEN THE VOTES WERE counted on Election Day 2016, Trump won the Electoral College vote, but Hillary won the popular vote. That was enough to encourage diehard Hillary supporters to think that there yet may be a way to deny Trump the victory. Maybe one or more strategic recounts could tip the Electoral College vote to Hillary. Or maybe enough electors could be convinced that Trump was unfit to give Hillary the 270 electoral votes needed for victory.

Protests began almost immediately, with thousands of people marching on Trump Tower the day after the election. Protests continued in the days following the election as demonstrators took to the streets holding signs that said, "Not My President," the #NeverTrump rally cry, while Deep State operatives behind the scenes devised strategies that might block Trump from being inaugurated. In the weeks between Election Day on November 8, 2016, and Inauguration Day on January 20, 2017, the Deep State, together with Democratic Party operatives, dared to imagine that if Trump could be prevented from taking the oath of office, Hillary Clinton may yet be president.

Riots in the Streets

On November 10, 2016, Trump tweeted, "Just had a very open and successful presidential election. Now professional protestors, incited by the media, are protesting. Very unfair!" On November 11, 2016, the Associated Press reported that Portland, Oregon, was the epicenter of the anti-Trump riots spreading across the country, with some 4,000 protestors marching in Portland's downtown area, smashing windows and chanting "We reject the president-elect." As midnight approached, Portland police pushed back against the crowd, arresting 26 demonstrators as protestors threw rocks at them.[1] Similar gatherings occurred throughout the United States:

- In Denver, protesters managed to briefly shut down Interstate 25 as demonstrators made their way onto the freeway. Traffic was halted in the northbound and southbound lanes for about 30 minutes. Protesters also briefly shut down interstate highways in Minneapolis and Los Angeles.

- In San Francisco, high-spirited high school students marched through downtown, chanting "Not my president" and holding signs urging a Donald Trump eviction. Protestors waved rainbow banners and Mexican flags as bystanders high-fived the marchers from the sidelines.

- In New York City, a large group of demonstrators gathered outside Trump Tower on 5th Avenue, chanting angry slogans and waving banners bearing anti-Trump messages.

- In Philadelphia, protesters near city hall held signs bearing slogans like "Not Our President," "Trans against Trump," and "Make America Safe for All."

Three days after the election, the *Washington Post* reported that some 225 people had been arrested in anti-Trump protests, with at least 185 arrested in Los Angeles alone.[2] To Hillary's consternation, many of the people protesting in the streets had not even bothered to vote in the election. NBC's KGW in Portland, Oregon, reported that most of the 112 protestors arrested in that city did not vote in Oregon, according to state election records, with 79 of the demonstrators arrested either not registered to vote in the state or not recorded as having turned in a ballot.[3] An analysis conducted by the *Oregonian* newspaper in Portland investigating those arrested in ant-Trump demonstrations who did not vote revealed that at least one-third were out-of-state college students not eligible to vote in Oregon.[4]

Meanwhile, the conservative blogger known as the Gateway Pundit found proof that George Soros, the billionaire currency trader and investor whose Open Society Foundation is notorious for funding left-wing progressive causes, had funded anti-Trump leftist groups who were advertising on the internet to hire demonstrations in various cities across the United States.[5]

Hillary Blames Russia

On December 15, 2016, Hillary made a speech in New York to donors who the *New York Times* reported had collectively contributed roughly $1 billion to her 2016 presidential campaign, again blaming her defeat on a long-running strategy implemented by Russian president Vladimir Putin to discredit the fundamental tenants of American democracy. "Vladimir Putin himself directed the covert cyberattacks against our electoral system, against our democracy, apparently because he has a personal beef against me," Clinton said. "He is determined not only to score a point against me but also undermine our democracy."[6]

Clinton acted as if Trump's collusion with Russia and WikiLeaks was a proven fact. "This is part of a long-drawn strategy to cause us to doubt ourselves and to create the circumstances in which Americans either wittingly or unwittingly will begin to cede their freedoms to a much more powerful state," Clinton insisted. "This is an attack on our country."[7] What's important to remember here is that while WikiLeaks did obtain emails from the DNC and from Podesta, it has never been proven—in either case—that the Russians themselves hacked the DNC, nor has it been proven that WikiLeaks was working with the Russians.

On December 16, 2016, Assange made another public appearance in an interview conducted by Sean Hannity that was first broadcast on Hannity's national radio show and subsequently broadcast that night on Hannity's Fox News television show. Assange made clear that Russia did not provide the Podesta emails or the DNC emails to WikiLeaks. He insisted the source of the email leaks "was not a state party," denying that they came from any government. "We're unhappy that we felt that we needed to even say that it wasn't a state party," he said.

Finally, Assange pushed back against Hillary's accusations. "Normally, we say nothing at all," Assange told Hannity. "We have a conflict of interests. We have an excellent reputation, a strong interest in protecting our sources, and so we never say anything about them, never ruling anyone in or anyone out. Sometimes we do it, but we don't like to do it. We have another interest here that is maximizing the impact of our publications. So in order to protect a distraction attack against our publications, we've had to come out and say, 'No, it's not a state party. Stop trying to distract in that way and pay attention to the content of the publication.'"

When Hannity suggested that the leak came from a disgruntled source within the DNC, possibly even within Podesta's office, Assange sidestepped, refusing to answer the question, in direct contrast to the way in which he vociferously denied that the source was Russia.[8]

Yet on December 18, 2016, 10 days after the election, Podesta repeated the "Russia collusion" theory in an interview conducted by host Chuck Todd on NBC's Sunday morning show *Meet the Press*.

In response to Todd's direct questions, Podesta insisted the presidential election had been "distorted" by the Russian intervention. Asked if the election was a "free and fair" election, Podesta railed against Putin. "I think the Russians clearly intervened in the election. And . . . now we know that . . . the CIA, the director of national intelligence, [and] the FBI all agree that the Russians intervened to help Trump and that as they have noted this week, NBC first revealed that Vladimir Putin was personally involved with that," he insisted. Pressed by Todd to directly answer whether the election was "free and fair," Podesta accused Russia of wanting Hillary Clinton to lose. "A foreign adversary directly intervened into our Democratic institution and tried to tilt the election to Donald Trump. I think that if you look back and see what happened over the course of the last few weeks, you see the way the votes broke, you know," Podesta replied. "I was highly critical of the way the FBI—particularly the FBI director—managed the situation with respect to the Russian engagement versus Hillary Clinton's emails."[9] Republican defenders of Trump pushed back against Hillary and Podesta, suggesting that the "Russian collusion" narrative was a Democratic Party invention that was being disseminated by the Deep State.

Then on December 18, 2016, Representative Peter King (Republican, New York), a member of the House intelligence community, pushed back against the "Russian collusion" meme. King insisted that CIA Director Brennan was orchestrating a "hit job" against president-elect Donald Trump by leaking information suggesting Russia was behind the hacking of Podesta's emails to the press, despite having "no evidence" to prove the assertion. "And that's what infuriates me about this . . . we have John Brennan, supposedly John Brennan, leaking to the *Washington Post*—to a biased newspaper like the *New York Times*—findings and conclusions that he's not telling the intelligence community," King said in an appearance on ABC's *This Week* Sunday show. "It seems like, to me, there should be an investigation with what the Russians did but also an investigation of John Brennan and the hit job he seems to be orchestrating against the president-elect," he insisted.[10]

Though unconfirmed, reports circulated that the Obama administration's director of national intelligence, James Clapper, held a meeting in his last days in office to float the idea of going to a Supreme Court justice to block Trump's inauguration on the premise that he only won because he colluded with Russia to hack Podesta emails that Russia leaked to WikiLeaks. "Clapper discussed blocking the inauguration on the grounds that Trump was an illegitimate president due to alleged Russian interference in the elections," Patrick Howley, a writer for BigLeaguePolitics .com, reported. Supposedly, a high-level member of the intelligence community who witnessed the meeting reported that Clapper discussed going to one of the three female Supreme Court justices to make the case that the alleged Russian interference could invalidate Trump's claim to the presidency.[11]

"Hamilton Electors" Urge Electoral College "Vote-Switching" Scheme

Perhaps the most desperate last-ditch effort to block Trump from the White House was organized by a group of citizens calling themselves "Hamilton Electors." The scheme involved unearthing obscure arguments from the Federalist Papers in a twisted attempt to argue that the Electoral College was created to keep a "scoundrel" like Trump from becoming president. "We honor Alexander Hamilton's vision that the Electoral College should, when necessary, act as a Constitutional failsafe against those lacking the qualifications from becoming President," the Hamilton Electors website proclaimed. "In 2016 we're dedicated to putting political parties aside and putting America first. Electors have already come forward calling upon other Electors from both red and blue states to unite behind a Responsible Republican candidate for the good of the nation."[12]

The goal of the Hamilton Electors was to convince enough of the 538 members of the Electoral College, scheduled to meet in their state capitals on December 19, 2016, to switch their votes to prevent Trump from getting the 270 electoral votes needed to be elected president. As freelance journalist Lilly O'Donnell pointed out in an article published on November 21, 2016, in the *Atlantic*, Michael Baca of Colorado and Bret Ciafolo of Washington State were the two Democratic electors who called themselves "Hamilton Electors."[13] The two Democrats formed the Hamilton

Electors in the hope of creating a national movement aimed at throwing the 2016 election into the House of Representatives. Still, given that Republicans controlled the House in 2016, the most the Hamilton Electors could have hoped to accomplish would have been to delegitimize Trump's victory by getting enough electors to switch their votes.

Baca and Ciafolo argued that Alexander Hamilton was right in Federalist Paper Number 68, in which he wrote that the Electoral College was deemed necessary because choosing a president by popular vote would give the most populated states, like New York and California today, an unfair advantage that would fail to account for the choices of lesser populated states.[14] The Hamilton Electors hoped to emphasize Hamilton's argument that "the office of President will never fall to the lot of any man who is not in an eminent degree endowed with the requisite qualifications." The point was that Trump should be denied the victory because he lacked the moral qualifications to be president—a fact the Hamilton Electors thought had been affirmed by Hillary winning the popular vote. To be successful, the Hamilton Electors would have had to convince 37 electors committed to voting for Trump to vote for someone else—a nearly impossible feat to accomplish.

As the Hamilton Electors' plan gained publicity in the mainstream media, the electors in Colorado and Washington State began to promote the idea that renegade electors should vote for a moderate Republican candidate, such as Republican governor John Kasich of Ohio. Kasich, a former GOP presidential candidate, sat out the Republican National Convention in Cleveland as an expression of his opposition to Trump.

In their best-case scenario, the Hamilton Electors dreamed of uniting 135 Republican and 135 Democratic electors behind Kasich, thus securing the presidency for a moderate Republican. In their fallback strategy, the Hamilton Electors plotted to convince 37 of the Republican electors in states that voted for Trump to switch their votes to Kasich, throwing the election into the House of Representatives. Their thought was that the GOP leadership in the House might be willing to twist the arms of Republican House members to vote for Kasich instead of Trump, a strategy designed to secure the presidency for the GOP while at the same time dumping Trump.

As December 19 approached—the day set for the electors to meet in their various state capitals—Republican members of the Electoral College faced intense pressure, including personal harassment and death threats, as pro-Hillary and anti-Trump forces combined in their desperate attempt to keep Trump out of the White House.[15] The bullying from the Trump haters was nearly overwhelming, with some electors receiving as many as 50,000 emails in the run-up to December 19, clogging their electronic devices with unwanted anti-Trump venom. Before the electors met to vote, a Harvard University group backed by constitutional law professor Lawrence Lessig got into the act, offering free legal advice to electors deciding to change their votes.[16]

Despite all the media hoopla, the "block Trump" Electoral College scheme was as dismal a failure as Jill Stein's ill-conceived re-count maneuver. In the end, Trump received 304 electoral votes to Clinton's 227—two fewer than he earned on November 8—with more electors going rogue and defecting from Clinton than defected from Trump.

CHAPTER 5

Democrats Go Hard-Left

Instead of seeking support from the center of the political spectrum, [the Democratic Party] has moved ever leftward, embracing positions that leave millions of Americans feeling left out.

—Erich Reimer, December 2017

WHEN THE MOVE TO deny Trump an Electoral College victory failed, Democrats and their supporters turned their attention away from the Clintons, resolving not just to resist Trump but to complete the hard-left take-over of the Democratic Party. They now wanted to set the stage for gaining a leftist majority to retake Congress in 2018 in the quest to find another Obama-like charismatic radical to retake the White House in 2020.

Once Trump was inaugurated, the Democrats' goal shifted to impeaching Trump, removing him from office by invoking the 25th Amendment, or forcing him to resign, with Pence then becoming president. In fact, Democrats were calling for Trump's impeachment even before he was inaugurated. Dozens of Democratic lawmakers refused to attend his inauguration. The Trump presidency was under siege almost immediately after he took the oath, setting the stage for the Deep State strategy that would not give Trump a moment to breathe. The Democrats eyed a repeat of Jimmy Carter's defeat of Gerald Ford in 1976 following Nixon's resignation on August 9, 1974, when Nixon preferred resignation to almost certain impeachment and removal from office over Watergate.

"Blowing Up the White House"

Protesting Donald Trump's presidency, famed singer Madonna gave a profanity-laced address in Washington, DC, on January 21, 2017, to a Women's March crowd estimated at 500,000 strong—a number various mainstream media reports argued was twice the number that had attended Trump's inauguration the day before. "Yes, I'm angry. Yes, I'm outraged," Madonna said, expressing her dismay at what the mainstream media accounts described as the "shocking electoral college win of minority President Donald Trump."[1]

Women in the protest march wore pink "pussy hats" knitted to display prominent feline ears. The hats symbolized opposition to a conversation recorded on a bus between Trump and Billy Bush, then host of *Access Hollywood*. A recording of that conversation was leaked to the *Washington Post* and published on Friday, October 7, 2016—two days before the second presidential debate. In that conversation, which Trump did not suspect was being recorded, Trump can be heard boasting in terms crude even in a locker room about grabbing women by their sexual organs.

Predictably, the mainstream media discounted Trump's apology as well as his counterargument: while his words were foolish and inappropriate, Bill Clinton lost his law license for much worse—namely, for lying about sexual advances he made toward Paula Jones, then an Arkansas state employee, when Clinton was governor of Arkansas. The height of Madonna's protest speech came when she cautioned that women would face "a new age of tyranny" under President Trump, adding the following incendiary language: "Yes, I've thought an awful lot about blowing up the White House. But I know this won't change anything. We cannot fall into despair."

Madonna attempted to explain away her obvious threat to the president by placing her protest in the context of love. "Welcome the revolution of love," she said. "To the rebellion. To our refusal as women to accept this new age of tyranny. We're not just women in danger, but all marginalized people." Responding to the estimated five million that took part in the 2017 Women's March protests nationwide, President Trump tweeted, "Watched protests yesterday but was under the impression that we just had an election! Why didn't these people vote? Celebs hurt cause badly."[2]

Despite making women's issues the centerpiece of her campaign, Hillary Clinton lost the votes of white women overall and struggled to win the votes of women without a college education in swing states including Ohio, Wisconsin, Michigan, and Pennsylvania—all states President Obama won in 2008 and 2012.[3] The real importance of the 2017 Women's March was that it signaled the degree to which the base of the Democratic Party was moving toward the far-left. The "pussy protesters" in the nation's streets after the election were radical feminists—new feminists of the hard-left who were angry not only about the economic inequality of women but about the white male privilege they believe is at the core of American capitalist oppression.

The women Hillary needed for victory might have voted for Bernie Sanders, but they were not impressed by Hillary Clinton. For these radical feminists, Clinton was a part of the past—a past dominated by too many six-figure fees paid to her by Goldman Sachs for her Wall Street speeches, a past tarnished by Clinton Foundation financial scandals and pay-to-play allegations. Hillary's past was truly ridden with scandal; she could not explain why Ambassador Chris Stevens had died at Benghazi or why she had refused to use the secure email devices provided by the State Department that were required to comply with national security laws.

Truthfully, there was much in Hillary's past that remained questionable and difficult to explain, from her being fired as a Watergate attorney to her role in Whitewater, or from the death of Vince Foster to the fact that Hillary's billing file from the Rose Law Firm were found squirreled away in a closet in the White House private residence. Add to this her husband's sexual escapades, plus a dozen other scandals that had plagued Hillary's career since she first stepped onto the public stage.

With Hillary's loss to Trump, the hard-left had only one objective, and Madonna captured it particularly well: "blow up the White House." While Madonna's supporters insisted that she did not mean this threat literally, Madonna's inability to accept Donald Trump as president triggered the hard-left's determination to impair his presidency with incessant resistance and obstruction. "Crooked Hillary" might have lost the election, but the hard-left's vision of completing Obama's "fundamental transformation of America" had only just begun.

Now with Hillary a "two-time loser" in presidential elections, Democrats could promote candidates from within the party's hard-left ranks who supported the radical left's agenda on issues ranging from open borders to same-sex marriage and tilting foreign policy to favor Islam over Israel.

Democratic National Committee Chooses New Leadership

On February 25, 2017, the Democratic National Committee chose an Obama administration insider, former labor secretary Tom Perez, to be DNC chair, tasked with rebuilding the Democratic National Party after Hillary Clinton's devastating loss. Perez has the type of radical, activist past that appeals to the Bill Ayers's hard-left wing of the Democratic Party. From 1995 to 2000, Perez served on the board of Casa of Maryland, a Hispanic advocacy group also affiliated with the radical national organization La Raza—the open-borders group that has for generations led the charge for illegal immigrants to be granted amnesty.

George Soros, Tom Perez, and the Politics of Chaos

Taking a page from the race riots and the violent Vietnam War protests of the 1960s and early 1970s, hard-left billionaire George Soros appears determined to escalate his campaign to destroy America by openly funding the politics of chaos.

On August 14, 2015, the *Washington Times* documented that Soros had funded—to the tune of some $33 million—the leftist groups that ignited violent riots in Ferguson, Missouri, a year earlier, with activists bussed to Ferguson by a host of far-left groups funded by Soros in Chicago, New York, and Washington.[4] With the decision of the Democratic National Party on February 25,

2017, to appoint Perez—an Obama administration official who had served both in the leadership of the DOJ's Civil Rights Division and as secretary of labor—as its new chair, Soros and his Open Society Foundation were positioned to advance Obama's implementation of the Saul Alinsky strategy designed to rub raw social tensions over race, immigration, and discrimination.

Soros and Perez have had a considerable history together. On May 15–16, 2014, Soros's Open Society hosted then secretary of labor Perez at its board meeting in New York City. Among the questions for Perez recommended by the staff of Soros's Open Society Foundation were these: "What is Department of Labor's role in the implementation of DACA [Deferred Action for Childhood Arrivals] and the intersection of DACA and workforce development issues? What can be done to ensure full implementation of DACA?" DACA was the program President Obama established by executive order that allowed children who entered the United States illegally before 2007, while they were yet less than 16 years old, to receive a two-year period of deferred action and deportation and a green card permit to work, provided they were enrolled in school (or honorably discharged from the military) and had no criminal record.

On June 23, 2016, the Supreme Court deadlocked in a 4–4 tie, leaving in place an appeals court record that blocked the Obama administration from making DACA permanent and expanding the DACA privileges to parents of DACA-eligible youths. On September 5, 2017, President Trump ended the DACA program by executive order, urging Congress to pass a replacement before ordering DACA to phase out all protections in six months. Perez's reaction to Trump's decision was expectedly angry. "Donald Trump has secured his legacy as a champion for cruelty," Perez said. "First, he took away protections for immigrant parents. Now he's going after the children. Rescinding DACA is the latest tactic in the Republican playbook to promote hate and discrimination."[5]

Democrats radicalized by Senator George McGovern's antiwar agenda in 1968, however, were the precursors for a Democratic Party today willing to unleash violent anarchists to advance their hard-left agenda. For decades, Soros has been behind the move to shift the Democratic Party from the liberal agenda of John F. Kennedy and Hubert Humphrey of the 1960s to the hard-left revolutionary agenda of Weather Underground terrorist bomber Bill Ayers. In this radical transformation of the Democratic Party, Soros has been ready to pour hundreds of millions of dollars into training rabble-rousers and political operatives to transition away from the disciplined "civil disobedience" civil rights marches led by Martin Luther King Jr. in the 1960s to the anarchistic violence of the Occupy, Antifa, and Black Lives Matter movements that we experience today. Now with Perez and Ellison at the head of the DNC, Soros is positioned to transform the Democratic Party into an even more radical organization—one that prevents Trump-supporting members of Congress from holding peaceful town hall meetings, while anarchists marching in the streets break windows, block traffic, and shout obscenities.

CHAPTER 6

The Deep State Sets a Trap

At a conference in mid-July, Barack Obama's CIA director, John Brennan, remarked that executive branch officials have an "obligation . . . to refuse to carry out" outrageous or anti-democratic orders from President Donald Trump.

Michael Crowley, Politico, September 2017

To REMOVE TRUMP FROM the presidency, the Deep State had no choice but to gain political control over the Justice Department. Should a Trump-appointed attorney general begin investigating Democrats in the Obama administration, the mainstream media promotion of the Russian collusion narrative would be derailed.

With a Trump-loyalist appointed as the attorney general, the Department of Justice could turn the tables and begin investigating Hillary Clinton and John Podesta for the payments they received for selling US military technology to Russia under Secretary Clinton's "reset" strategy. From there, the investigation could examine Secretary Clinton's role in the Clinton Foundation pay-to-play scandal with Canadian entrepreneur Frank Giustra that ended up with Russia owning some 20 percent of all US uranium production.

The appointment of Senator Jeff Sessions to the position of attorney general proved a profound disappointment and setback for Trump when Sessions decided to recuse himself from the DOJ investigation into Russian election collusion with the Trump campaign.

The moment Trump blew up against Sessions for recusing himself, Democratic Party leaders including Chuck Schumer and Nancy Pelosi went public, notifying Trump that his firing of Sessions would be sufficient to precipitate bringing impeachment charges against him in the House. With Trump blocked politically from firing Sessions, the Deep State maneuvered to have Robert Mueller, a Deep State operative who had served both the

Bush and the Obama administrations as the attorney general from 2001 to 2013, appointed as special counsel.

John Brennan, Obama's CIA Handler, Intervenes in Election

New York Republican Representative Peter King, a member of the House intelligence community, was among the first to insist that CIA Director John Brennan was responsible for orchestrating a "hit job" against president-elect Donald Trump by going around the intelligence community and leaking information to the press suggesting that Russia was behind the hack of Clinton campaign chairman John Podesta. "And that's what infuriates me about this is that we have John Brennan—supposedly John Brennan—leaking to the *Washington Post*, to a biased newspaper like the *New York Times*, findings and conclusions that he's not telling the intelligence community," King said in an appearance on ABC's *This Week* on December 18, 2016. "It seems like to me [that] there should be an investigation with what the Russians did, but also an investigation of John Brennan and the hit job he seems to be orchestrating against the president-elect," King insisted.[1]

Since before the 2008 election, as noted earlier, Brennan appears to have been Barack Obama's CIA "handler." In 2008, Obama was one of the three presidential candidates involved who had his passport file breached on three separate occasions, with the first occurring on January 9, followed by separate violations on February 21 and March 14. The *New York Times* noted that the two offending State Department contract employees who were fired had worked for Stanley Inc., a company based in Arlington, Virginia, while the reprimanded worker continued to be employed by the Analysis Corporation of McLean, Virginia. The newspaper gave no background on either corporation other than to note that Stanley Inc. did "computer work for the government."[2]

On March 22, 2008, the *Washington Times* reported that
Obama's passport breach traced back the Analysis Corporation
of McLean, Virginia. John Brennan, a former CIA agent who
was then serving as an advisor on intelligence and foreign policy to then senator Obama's presidential campaign, headed the
Analysis Corporation.[3] Although the State Department prom-
ised a full-scale investigation at the time, the public was kept in
the dark. In July 2008, the State Department's Office of Inspector
General issued a 104-page investigative report on the passport
breach incidents involving the presidential candidates, stamped
"Sensitive but Unclassified," that was so heavily redacted as to be
near worthless to the public.[4]

Investigative reporter Kenneth Timmerman claimed a well-
placed but unnamed source told him that the real point of the
passport breach incidents was to cauterize the Obama file, removing from it any information that could prove damaging to his eli-
gibility to be president. According to this theory, the breaches of
then presidential candidate John McCain's and Hillary Clinton's
files were done for misdirection purposes—to create confusion
and to suggest that the motives of the perpetrators were attrib-
utable entirely to innocent curiosity.[5] Brennan was brought into
the White House as deputy security advisor for homeland security and counterterrorism before being appointed by President
Obama to head the CIA in 2013.

On February 13, 2010, in a speech to New York University
School of Law students that the White House posted on You-
Tube, Brennan, then the assistant to the president for homeland
security and counterterrorism, included a lengthy statement in
Arabic that he did not translate for his English-speaking audience. Noting that he was an undergraduate at the American
University in Cairo in the 1970s, Brennan proceeded to use only
the Arabic name, Al-Quds, when referring to Jerusalem. Brennan commented that during his 25 years in government, he
spent considerable time in the Middle East as a political officer

with the State Department and as a CIA station chief in Saudi Arabia. "In Saudi Arabia, I saw how our Saudi partners fulfilled their duty as custodians of the two holy mosques in Mecca and Medina," he said. "I marveled at the majesty of the Hajj and the devotion of those who fulfilled their duty as Muslims of making that pilgrimage."[6]

Brennan persisted in pushing the "Russian collusion" meme against the Trump campaign even after various other heads of intelligence and law enforcement organizations with the federal government testified, often under oath, that there was "no evidence" to prove that contention.

On May 8, 2017, Director of National Intelligence James Clapper told a Senate judiciary subcommittee under oath that he had not seen any evidence of collusion between the Trump campaign and Russian officials. Only weeks earlier, Clapper told *NBC News*, "We did not include any evidence in our report, and I say, 'our,' that's NSA, FBI and CIA, with my office, the Director of National Intelligence, that had anything, that had any reflection of collusion between members of the Trump campaign and the Russians. There was no evidence of that included in our report."[7]

But when Representative Trey Gowdy grilled former CIA director Brennan at a House Intelligence Committee hearing on May 23, 2017, if he had any hard evidence of collusion between Trump campaign officials and Russia, Brennan answered cryptically, "I don't do evidence." When Gowdy pressed Brennan that *assessment* is the intelligence tradecraft word for *evidence*, Brennan finally admitted that the CIA had no evidence of collusion, but he did so in a way that intentionally suggested there was a lot of smoke, even if no fire had been found: "I don't know whether or not such collusion—and that's your term, such collusion existed. I don't know. But I know that there was a sufficient basis of information and intelligence that required further investigation by the bureau to determine whether or not U.S. persons were actively conspiring, colluding with Russian officials."[8]

Deep State Maneuvers to Appoint Special Counsel

On March 2, 2017, Attorney General Jeff Sessions recused himself from investigations into Russian interference in the 2016 elections after Democrats in Congress, led by House Minority Leader Nancy Pelosi, pressed that Sessions may not have fully disclosed in his confirmation hearings conversations with Russian ambassador Sergey Kislyak.[9]

On May 9, 2017, President Trump fired James Comey as FBI director based on the recommendation of Attorney General Sessions and Deputy Attorney General Rod J. Rosenstein. "I cannot defend the director's handling of the conclusion of the investigation of Secretary Clinton's emails," Rosenstein wrote in a letter released by the White House, "and I do not understand his refusal to accept the nearly universal judgment that he was mistaken."

Almost immediately, the Deep State reacted with indignation, with Senate Minority Leader Chuck Schumer of New York charging that by firing Comey, Trump was attempting to cover up the Russia investigation.[10] Comey and the FBI had just opened a grand jury investigation in Virginia that had issued subpoenas for records related to President Trump's decision to fire national security advisor Michael T. Flynn for misleading Vice President Mike Pence about the extent of his contacts with the Russian ambassador during the presidential transition.[11]

Then on May 17, 2017, eight days after Trump fired Comey, Rosenstein, as acting attorney general—given Sessions's decision to recuse himself in the Russian investigation—appointed former FBI director Robert Mueller to serve as special counsel, charged with investigating "any links and/or coordination between the Russian government and individuals associated with the campaign of Donald J Trump." Rosenstein's letter was so broad as to include "any matter" arising from the Russian collusion investigation.[12]

By firing Comey, Trump fell into a Deep State plan engineered by Democratic Party operatives to put the president under an investigation with virtually unlimited scope, unlimited completion deadline, and unlimited funding. During the Clinton administration, Rosenstein joined the team of prosecutors working under Independent Counsel Kenneth W. Starr's investigation of Hillary and Bill Clinton's real-estate holdings in the Whitewater affair—an investigation that concluded with no indictments being filed against the Clintons. Appointed in 2005 by President George W. Bush to be the US attorney for Maryland, Rosenstein was the only US attorney appointed by Bush who was asked to stay on by President Obama during his eight-year term.[13]

Although furious at Sessions, Trump realized that the Deep State had set a trap, pushing the Russia collusion narrative to the point where Sessions felt pressured to recuse himself. With Sessions removed from the Russia collusion investigation, Rosenstein, a long-term Department of Justice operative favorable to the Democrats, took the opportunity to appoint Robert Mueller, another long-term Deep State operative, as special counselor. As special counselor, Mueller was in a position to bring criminal obstruction of justice charges against Trump for firing Comey as well as charges that Trump had colluded with the Russians to win the election.

Rosenstein, Comey, and Mueller all shared a history of working in the Department of Justice that traced back to the Clinton administration, with all three having worked on FBI investigations that ultimately resulted in exonerating the Clintons from any wrongdoing—a history that stretched back to Whitewater, the real estate fraud that involved Hillary and Bill Clinton when Bill was an Arkansas governor and included, as we shall soon see, other Clinton scandals such as the Marc Rich pardon. With Mueller appointed, the Democrats in Congress launched threats of impeachment if Trump should fire Sessions as a prelude to firing Mueller.

Truthfully, the hiring and firing of the FBI director, the attorney general, and any independent prosecutor appointed (even one disguised by the more innocuous-sounding title of "special coun-sel") are all within the authority of the president. Yet the Deep State devised the mainstream media narrative such that Trump's firing Comey was construed as evidence that he was obstruct-ing justice in the Russian collusion probe. The Deep State, with the willing cooperation of the mainstream media, was willing to elevate that narrative to the impeachment level if Trump dared complete the job of protecting himself by firing not only Comey but also Rosenstein, Sessions, and Mueller.

James Comey, Robert Mueller, and Loretta Lynch—All Clinton-Fixers

As suggested previously, FBI Director James Comey is a Clinton-fixer with a long history of running interference within the Department of Justice to make sure the Clintons are never prosecuted—a loyalty that the Clintons have repaid in corporate board appointments that have earned Comey millions of dollars. As noted earlier, Comey's involvement in protecting Hillary goes back to the mid-1990s and the Whitewater scandal. The same holds true for both Robert Mueller, who served as the head of the FBI from 2001 to 2013, and for Loretta Lynch, who served as the attorney general from 2015 to 2017, the successor to Obama confidant Eric Holder.

In January 2016, Judicial Watch released 246 pages of previ-ously undisclosed internal memos obtained by a Freedom of Information Act (FOIA) request from Ken Starr's Office of Inde-pendent Counsel investigation in 1998 that prove Department of Justice prosecutors had evidence that Hillary Clinton and her associate Webb Hubbell at the Rose Law Firm in Little Rock, Arkansas, were guilty of criminal fraud in the Whitewater real estate affair.[14] In April 1995, Hickman Ewing, the chief deputy to Kenneth Starr, drafted an indictment of Hillary Clinton, alleging that she provided false information and withheld information from both the Senate and the Independent Counsel investigating

Watergate.[15] Comey was among those investigating the White-water scandal responsible for convincing Department of Justice prosecutors to decline prosecuting the then first lady supposedly because of the perceived difficulty of persuading a jury to convict a public figure as widely known as Clinton.

Comey and Mueller combined to sanitize the Marc Rich pardon. Consider the following:

- From 1987 to 1993, Comey worked in the US attorney's office for the Southern District of New York, where he served as the DOJ prosecutor who oversaw the prosecution of Marc Rich, the billionaire oil trader convicted of tax fraud and trading with Iran during the embassy hostage crisis.[16]

- In 2001, when Bill Clinton decided on his last day in office to pardon Marc Rich, Comey as then incoming US attorney for the Southern District of New York was enthusiastic about the proposed investigative plan looking into the pardon that was proposed by the Justice Department.[17]

- In 2005, then attorney general Mueller made the decision to close the FBI grand jury investigation into the Marc Rich pardon that Comey had convened in 2001, despite public outcry over the evidence that Rich's ex-wife had donated to Hillary Clinton's Senate campaign.

Mueller and Comey also combined to give Sandy Berger a pass on stealing sensitive Clinton administration–related documents from the National Archives.

- In 2004, Comey, then serving as a deputy attorney general in the Justice Department, limited the criminal investigation of Sandy Berger so as to protect anyone in the former Clinton administration who may have coordinated with Berger in his removal and destruction of classified records from the National Archives.[18]

· At that time, Berger was under criminal investigation by the Justice Department for removing various classified documents from the National Archives that should have been turned over to the independent commission then investigating the 9/11 terror attacks and for removing handwritten notes he made while reviewing the documents.

· On April 1, 2005, with Mueller serving as the head of the FBI, Berger was allowed to plead guilty to a misdemeanor charge of intentionally removing documents from the National Archives and destroying some of them, for which he was fined $50,000 and sentenced to 100 hours of community service and probation for two years, with his national security license stripped for two years.

No one else was prosecuted for the crime, even though Berger allegedly stole the documents to protect the Clintons.

In 2016, Berger surfaced once again when his email correspondence advising Secretary of State Clinton was found on Hillary's private email server.[19] Neither Comey's FBI nor Lynch's DOJ took any steps to bring Hillary Clinton to justice.

Cheryl Mills, Sandy Berger, and a host of additional Obama administration officials were involved in Hillary's use of a private email server to transmit classified State Department documents in what should have been judged a clear violation of national security laws. Even the disclosure that President Obama used a pseudonym to communicate with Secretary of State Clinton over her private email server was covered up by a Deep State and lapdog mainstream media uninterested in exposing crimes committed by Democrats. So it should not surprise us that James Comey, Robert Mueller, and Loretta Lynch were all involved in the 2012 HSBC scandal in which the bank managed to avoid criminal charges in a massive money-laundering scandal for which the bank paid a $1.9 billion fine to the US government.

From 2002 to 2003, Comey held the position of US attorney for the Southern District of New York, the same position held by Lynch. On March 4, 2013, Comey joined the HSBC board of directors, agreeing to serve as an independent nonexecutive director and a member of the bank's Financial System Vulnerabilities Committee, positions he held until he resigned on August 3, 2013, to become the head of the FBI.[20]

Loretta Lynch, then the US attorney for the Eastern District of New York, was responsible for negotiating the "deferred prosecution" settlement that allowed the HSBC to pay the $1.9 billion fine, admitting "willful criminal conduct" in exchange for dropping criminal investigations and prosecutions of HSBC directors, including Comey.[21] Throughout the time the HSBC was being investigated for money laundering, Robert Mueller headed the FBI. The investigations by the FBI and the Senate Permanent Investigating Subcommittee made clear that the HSBC had played a key role laundering money for drug cartels in Mexico and terrorists in the Middle East, with Deep State knowledge and complicity.[22]

By allowing the HSBC to avoid criminal charges despite pleading guilty to money-laundering violations for both the Mexican drug cartel and Middle Eastern radical Islamic terrorist groups, Comey, Muller, Lynch, and then attorney general Eric Holder were all playing major roles as Deep State operatives. It is impossible to imagine that with the surveillance capabilities of the US government, the HSBC got away for years with laundering hundreds of billions of dollars in drug and terrorist cash without the knowledge of the NSA, the CIA, the US Treasury, the Comptroller of the Currency, and a dozen other federal agencies that one way or another monitor large movements of money through the banking system. The reality is that without the complicity of criminal banks in money-laundering activities, drug cartels and terrorist organizations could not function. Drug cartel criminals and terrorists would not get far if their only means of utilizing money was reduced to transporting containers packed with $100 bills.

The Deep State secret, as alluded to in earlier chapters, is that the CIA has been involved since its inception both in operating the international trade in illicit drugs and in creating, financing, and arming various terrorist organizations around the globe. For those skeptical of the CIA's continuing role in the international drug trade, ask yourself why the production of heroin poppies in Afghanistan was reversed from record lows under the Taliban to record highs under the watchful eye of the US military.

- In its quarterly report to the US Congress on April 30, 2017, the special inspector general for Afghanistan Reconstruction acknowledged that despite an $8.5 billion counternarcotics campaign by the US government, opium production increased 43 percent in 2016, setting new records, with the gross value of opiates produced at $1.56 billion, or the equivalent of 7.4 percent of Afghanistan's gross domestic product (GDP) in 2015, while poppy eradication hit a 10-year low and was "nearly imperceptible."[23]

- Ironically, in 2001, the United Nation's drug control program was forced to report that after one season, the Taliban had managed to wipe out the world's largest opium-poppy crop, located in Afghanistan, responsible for supplying about three-quarters of the world's opium and most of the opium reaching Europe.[24]

Serving on the HSBC was not Comey's only chance to cash in on his faithful service to the Deep State in his various FBI and DOJ assignments. From 2005 to 2010, before serving on the HSBC board, Comey served as general counsel and senior vice president for Lockheed Martin, a major US military contractor—jobs for which Comey earned $6 million.

In 2010, Lockheed Martin joined the Clinton Global Initiative and won 17 contracts from the State Department, which at the time was headed by secretary of state Hillary Clinton. Comey's brother, Peter Comey, was also found working at the Washington law firm DLA Piper, which prepares Clinton Foundation taxes in addition to the 2015 audit on the Clinton Foundation, the same firm that is listed as one of Hillary Clinton's top 10 all-time career campaign donors. "These relationships, though egregious, are symptomatic of the brazen culture of crony capitalism that exists in our nation's capital," noted investigative reporter Patrick Howley in disclosing these interconnections. "The public usually is prevented from learning these kinds of things, with the mainstream media blocking information from coming out. Sunlight is the only remedy."[25]

In 1999, Cheryl Mills, then serving as White House counsel for President Bill Clinton, defended Clinton during his impeachment trial. She subsequently served as the senior advisor and special counsel to Hillary Clinton during the 2008 presidential campaign. Throughout Hillary's term as secretary of state, Mills served both as her legal counsel and as her chief of staff. Curiously, Sandy Berger, Loretta Lynch, and Cheryl Mills all worked as partners in the Washington law firm Hogan & Hartson—the law firm that prepared tax returns for the Clintons and was one of the biggest contributors in the legal industry to Hillary Clinton's 2008 presidential campaign.

- Berger worked as a partner in the Washington law firm Hogan & Hartson from 1973 to 1977 before taking a position as the deputy director of policy planning at the State Department in the Carter administration.

- When Carter lost his reelection bid, Berger returned to Hogan & Hartson, where he worked until he took leave in 1988 to act as foreign policy advisor in then governor Michael Dukakis's presidential campaign.

- When Dukakis was defeated, Berger returned to Hogan & Hartson until he became foreign policy advisor for Bill Clinton's presidential campaign in 1992.

- In 1999, President Bill Clinton nominated Lynch for the first of her two terms as US attorney for the Eastern District of New York, a position she held until she joined Hogan & Hartson in March 2002.

- In a press release issued on March 20, 2002, Hogan & Hartson, currently known as Hogan Lovells after a May 2010 merger with a London-based law firm, announced that Lynch had joined the firm's New York office as a partner in the Litigation Practice Group, focusing her law practice on commercial litigation, white-collar criminal defense, and corporate compliance issues.

- Lynch left Hogan & Hartson in 2010 after being nominated by President Obama for her second term as the US attorney for the Eastern District of New York, a position she held until President Obama nominated her on November 8, 2014, to replace Attorney General Eric Holder.

- An article published by the *American Lawyer* on April 8, 2008, noted that Hogan & Hartson was among Hillary Clinton's biggest financial supporters in the legal industry during her first presidential campaign. "Firm lawyers and staff have donated nearly $123,400 to her campaign so far, according to campaign contribution data from the Center for Responsive Politics," Nate Raymond observed in the article. "Christine Varney, a partner in Hogan's Washington, DC, office, served as chief counsel to the Clinton-Gore Campaign in 1992."[26]

- According to documents that Hillary Clinton's first presidential campaign made public in 2008, Hogan & Hartson's New York–based partner Howard Topaz was the tax lawyer who filed income tax returns for Bill and Hillary Clinton beginning in 2004.

· While there is no evidence that Lynch played a direct role either in the tax work done by the firm for the Clintons or in linking Hillary's private email server to MX Logic, the ethics of the legal profession hold all partners jointly liable for the action of other partners in the business. "If Hogan and Hartson previously represented the Clintons on tax matters, it is incumbent upon U.S. Attorney General Loretta Lynch to disclose what, if any, role she had in such tax matters," said Tom Fitton, president of Washington-based Judicial Watch.[27]

This should be enough to understand that key players trying to get Hillary Clinton elected as president in 2016 and conspiring to remove Donald Trump from the White House in 2017 all have interconnected personal histories that have crossed paths numerous times.

Comey, Mueller, Lynch, and Holder, together with a small group of Clinton confidants such as Cheryl Mills, have played repeated roles as Clinton-fixers who were not hesitant to extend their loyalty to Barack Obama. All worked in the interest of making sure Democratic Party high crimes and misdemeanors in the White House were excused. FBI and DOJ operatives favorable to the Democrats made sure investigations into Deep State crimes went nowhere, as evidenced by investigations that whitewashed Bill Clinton's pardoning of international criminal Marc Rich, giving Sandy Berger a slap on the wrist for stealing documents from the National Archives, and making sure HSBC money laundering for both drug cartels and international terrorists was punished only by a fine the bank could write off as the cost of being in the drug and terrorism businesses.

As long as Comey, Muller, and Lynch played their roles within the Department of Justice, Democratic Party operatives and Deep State counterparts, including John Brennan at the CIA, could continue to advance their globalist military-industrial complex goals unimpeded.

Is Jeff Sessions Compromised?

President Trump's frustration that Sessions could have blocked the appointment of a special counselor in the "Russian collusion" investigation had he not recused himself bubbled over with the added frustration that Sessions was apparently unwilling to investigate the Clintons. Once appointed as the attorney general, Sessions appeared to turn a blind eye to Clinton Foundation financial accounting irregularities. As previously noted, Sessions seemed equally unconcerned about the "pay-to-play" allegations regarding Canadian entrepreneur Frank Giustra and Secretary of State Clinton's role in the Uranium One deal. As initially exposed by Peter Schweizer in his 2015 book *Clinton Cash*, the Uranium One scandal resulted in Russia gaining control of some 20 percent of all US uranium in return for $145 million in contributions to the Clinton Foundation and hundreds of thousands of dollars in speaker fees for Bill Clinton.[28]

Trump was also infuriated that Sessions was not looking into the National Security Agency's (NSA) extensive electronic surveillance authorized by the Foreign Intelligence Surveillance Act (FISA) as well as the "unmasking" of Trump campaign officials' names to the mainstream media that the Obama administration had allowed. Trump was furious that Sessions did not follow up on charges that Hillary Clinton campaign officials had colluded with Ukrainian officials to sabotage Trump's campaign.[29]

The author can confirm from personal experience that Sessions as an attorney general refused to meet privately with anyone identified by Democratic Party operatives and their mainstream media lapdogs as "alt-right" radioactive. Those close to Sessions explained that he was concerned that Obama operatives yet in the NSA were conducting electronic surveillance that captured all his telephone and cell phone conversations as well as his emails.

Remarkably, Sessions believed that even as attorney general, he was under electronic surveillance by the NSA and the intelligence agencies, including the CIA. Sessions was also fearful that leaks from within his office would expose any meetings he had with conservatives and libertarians pressing for the DOJ to investigate Hillary and Obama. Simply put, Sessions did not want anyone appearing on his official DOJ calendar that might cause him embarrassment.

Shockingly, Sessions's paranoia that he was being spied on deterred him from taking any steps to meet with Trump loyalists, which he believed might have drawn Democratic Party mainstream media criticism. Sessions came to fear that he would lose his job if he dared to follow President Trump's repeated exhortations to investigate the Clintons and the Obamas.

How different this was from the Obama administration, where records prove that Robert Creamer, a veteran leftist political operative who founded the shady Democracy Partners, made 340 visits to the Obama White House, 45 of which included meetings with President Obama.[30]

Project Veritas's James O'Keefe had captured Creamer on hidden camera video, revealing Creamer's willingness to hire rabble-rousers and even the mentally ill to disrupt GOP functions. The truth is that Creamer had an open door to Obama's Oval Office despite his four-decade-long history as a Democratic operative who pleaded guilty in 2005 to charges of bank fraud and tax violations, recruited agitators—including union members, homeless people, and the mentally ill—to incite violence by provoking Trump supporters on camera at campaign stops.[31]

Clearly Barack Obama had nothing to fear from the NSA or the CIA as long as John Brennan was heading the CIA or from the Department of Justice as long as Eric Holder or Loretta Lynch was attorney general. With the White House staff loyal to Obama and the Democrats confident that they controlled a subservient and politically partisan mainstream media, Obama felt comfortable using the White House as his personal "dirty tricks" base of operations. Working under this cover, Obama felt he could rig the election in favor of Hillary Clinton, even if it meant encouraging the FBI and DOJ to conduct Foreign Intelligence Surveillance Court–ordered electronic surveillance of Trump campaign officials. Obama apparently went so far as to violate national security laws regarding the privacy rights of US citizens by unmasking the names of Trump campaign officials under surveillance and leaking that information to the press.

Sessions would investigate none of these improprieties. In his unwillingness to "drain the swamp," Sessions did nothing to remove Clinton and Obama holdovers from key positions within the FBI and DOJ bureaucracy. Additionally troublesome was that Sessions refrained from investigating IRS director Josh Koskinen, despite the role Koskinen played in the Tea Party.

During the Obama administration, Koskinen defended Lois Lerner when it was proven that Lerner, as head of the IRS Exempt Organizations Unit, had blackballed Tea Party patriot groups from obtaining tax-exempt 501(c)(3) or 501(c)(4) status. Instead of restructuring the IRS to remove its obvious political bias for the Democrats, Sessions shocked Trump supporters when he told Congressional Republicans on September 8, 2017, that he had no plans to bring any criminal charges against Lois Lerner, despite Lerner having taken the Fifth Amendment to avoid answering questions from Congress.[32] More about the IRS going scot-free later.

What worried Trump supporters was the possibility that as long as Sessions was the attorney general, the FBI and DOJ would continue to protect Democrats, even when Democrats were suspected of committing obvious criminal felonies in their pursuits of political power.

As 2017 came to an end, it appeared that the Deep State had not only trapped Trump into the appointment of Mueller but also prevented him from firing Sessions. Most troubling, the Deep

State appeared to have completed their control over the Trump Department of Justice by cowing Attorney General Sessions into believing that he was under constant Deep State surveillance, such that any steps he took to protect Trump by investigating Democrats would produce a flurry of leaks that the mainstream media would cover nonstop—at least until Sessions resigned.

PART 2

The Deep State's Plan to Remove Trump from Office

CHAPTER 7

The Trump Dossier

The real Russia scandal? [The] Clinton
campaign paid for the fake Russia dossier,
then lied about it and covered it up.

—Sarah Huckabee Sanders, October 2017

THE DEEP STATE EFFORT to politicize the US government bureaucracy requires that the FBI, Department of Justice, and IRS know which "enemies of the state" to target for harassment, civil and criminal investigations, tax audits, and criminal prosecutions. For this reason, the Deep State needs an intelligence-gathering operation that extends beyond the CIA and the myriad other military-affiliated secret intelligence gathering operations. The bureaucratic organization of choice is the National Security Agency (NSA).

Under the umbrella of the office of the director of national intelligence, the NSA has evolved into a massive surveillance operation with a secondary purpose not of screening for foreign national security threats as required by law but of keeping constant tabs on citizens and other residents of the United States that the Deep State feels may be a threat to the advancement of its global government objectives.

The Church Committee investigating US intelligence agencies in 1976 concluded that at that time, the FBI had developed more than 500,000 domestic intelligence files. Between 1953 and 1973, the FBI had opened nearly a quarter of a million first-class letters, while the CIA produced a computerized index containing the names of nearly 1.5 million US citizens. By 1967, the NSA was collecting information on thousands of Americans included on a "watch list" targeting peace groups, Black Power groups, as well as any organization or individuals believed to be in engaged in activities that may result in civil disturbances or otherwise subvert the national security of the United States.[1]

In his testimony to the Watergate Committee on June 27, 1973, John Dean first revealed that President Nixon had maintained an "enemies list" of political opponents. These individuals were targeted by the Nixon administration and harassed by the "available federal machinery." They were to be denied grant availability and federal contracts and hassled by IRS and FBI investigations, which would lead to possible prosecutions—any means the federal bureaucracy could invent and implement to make their lives difficult.

With the passage of the Patriot Act in the wake of the 9/11 terrorist attacks, the US surveillance agencies were granted new authority for domestic intelligence gathering. Revelations from whistleblowers, including Edward Snowden and William Binney, have made clear that under President Obama, domestic intelligence gathering aimed at keeping US citizens under surveillance had reached new heights.

Deep State Surveillance under President Obama

In 2013, Edward Snowden, a computer professional and a former CIA employee, stole thousands of classified records from the NSA that were ultimately made public by the *Guardian* in London, the *New York Times* and the *Washington Post* in the United States, and *Der Spiegel* in Germany. Snowden's disclosures exposed an NSA surveillance program known as PRISM, which involved the NSA tapping directly into the servers of nine internet firms, including Facebook, Google, Microsoft, Apple, AOL, SKYPE, YouTube, Paltalk, and Yahoo to track communications.[2] Snowden opened a floodgate of disclosures proving that the NSA under the Obama administration engaged in widespread domestic surveillance operations.

The NSA operates the PRISM program under Section 702 of the US Foreign Intelligence Surveillance Act (FISA), which allows electronic surveillance without obtaining a warrant if the spying is being done on internet communications, so long as a "significant" purpose of the surveillance is to gather "foreign intelligence information." The other program the NSA operates under Section 702 is known as "upstream" scanning, a process involving government searches of virtually all communications that flow abroad over the internet, including emails, chats, and web browsing traffic.[3] "If you send emails to friends abroad, message family members overseas, or browse websites outside of the United States, the NSA has almost certainly searched through your communications—and it has done so without a warrant," ACLU attorneys have warned. Whenever the NSA finds a communication that contains a "hit," the NSA stores that communication for long-term analysis, and the NSA may share those communications with the FBI for use in criminal investigations, the lawyers further cautioned.[4]

A report published by investigative journalist Sara Carter on May 23, 2011, revealed that President Obama "routinely violated" American privacy protections while scouring though overseas intercepts even after he issued a revised set of guidelines for Section 702 electronic surveillance in 2011. Carter reported that one out of every 20 searches seeking "upstream" internet data on Americans inside the NSA's so-called Section 702 database violated the safeguards Obama and his intelligence chiefs vowed to follow in 2011.[5] Carter also reported that the Obama administration engaged in illegally "unmasking" the names of US citizens who were identified by "US-person identifiers"—in other words, names—used to query results of upstream internet collections under Section 702.

According to Carter, the unmasked names of Trump campaign officials captured in Obama administration FBI and NSA surveillance of foreign nationals was widespread, regardless of whether the names of the Trump officials under investigation were obtained under US Foreign Intelligence Surveillance Court warrants or Section 702 electronic surveillance that did not require a court warrant. The unmasking allowed Obama administration officials with access to the FBI/NSA electronic surveillance tools to track insider information on the Trump campaign without the knowledge of the Trump campaign or the American people.

William Binney, an NSA whistleblower who was a leading code-breaker against the Soviet Union during the Cold War but resigned soon after 9/11, disgusted by Washington's moves toward mass surveillance, has suggested the NSA's goal is total control of the US population. "At least 80 percent of fibre-optic cables globally go via the US," Binney said. "This is no accident and allows the US to view all communication coming in. At least 80 percent of all audio calls, not just metadata, are recorded and stored in the US. The NSA lies about what it stores."[6] Snowden has also disclosed that the NSA has built a surveillance program capable of recording 100 percent of a foreign country's telephone calls, enabling the agency to rewind and review conversations for as long as a month after they happened. Snowden insists the voice interception program, called MYSTIC, began in 2009, with RETRO, the tool allowing "retrospective retrieval," implemented in full capacity against the first targeted nation in 2011.[7]

These disclosures strongly suggest that the NSA has the capability of recording and archiving all phone conversations as well as emails in the United States, even if the conversations are only recorded for possible subsequent review, possibly months or even years later. Given their history, it is apparent that the NSA and CIA only acknowledge increased implementation of domestic surveillance activities when they are caught. Why should US citizens trust that our conversations and emails are not being monitored by the government on a constant basis, whether or not we are targets of a legitimate federal law enforcement investigation? Binney cautions the Foreign Intelligence Surveillance Court fails to protect US citizens from NSA domestic surveillance. "The FISA court only has the government's point of view," Binney argued. "There are no other views for the judges to consider.

There have been at least 15–20 trillion constitutional violations for US domestic audiences and you can double that globally."[8]

A secret order issued in 2013 by the Foreign Intelligence Surveillance Court established to authorize FBI and NSA surveillance warrants issued against foreign spies operating in the United States provides evidence that US citizens were under massive secret government surveillance. Under this order, the NSA was given authority to demand that the telecommunications giant Verizon, on an "ongoing, daily basis," must hand over all telephone calls in its various systems, both within and between the United States and other countries. To be specific, the FISA order gave the NSA the ability with Verizon to collect and store data on call locations, duration, and identifiers on a dragnet basis, not limited to targeting specific individuals suspected of being foreign spies or agents of terrorist groups.[9] The order did not, however, authorize the NSA to record and collect the content of the calls. Subsequent three-month extensions of this FISA order allowed the NSA to collect this phone-record data from Verizon for years.

FISA electronic surveillance is particularly troubling when it identifies US citizens who are communicating with foreign nationals because the government does not have to prove probable cause of a crime to pursue electronic surveillance on a foreign national as long as the government has a "legitimate foreign-intelligence purpose" in the investigation.

The Deep State Lies, Denies US Citizens Are under Surveillance

On March 12, 2013, in an open session of the Senate Intelligence Committee, Senator Ron Wyden (Democrat, Oregon) asked National Intelligence Director James Clapper whether intelligence officials collect data on Americans. Clapper responded, "No, sir," adding after a hesitation, "Not wittingly. There are cases where they could inadvertently, perhaps, collect, but not wittingly." Given the evidence of the Verizon case, it appears Clapper was lying.

We know the NSA surveillance regularly captures US citizens when a US citizen shows up in a phone conversation with a foreign national under FISA-authorized electronic surveillance. This incidental involvement of a US citizen is perhaps what James Clapper meant when he qualified his answer to say, "Not wittingly."

Clinton Campaign and Democratic National Committee–Funded Fusion GPS "Russia Dossier" Attacking Trump

In October 2013, billionaire Wall Street GOP donor Paul Singer hired the US firm Fusion GPS to conduct opposition research on then presidential candidate Donald Trump. Singer had donated to the presidential campaigns of both Jeb Bush and Marco Rubio and was a major supporter of House Speaker Paul Ryan as well as the *Washington Free Beacon*, a conservative internet news website.[10]

Fusion GPS was cofounded in 2011 by three investigative journalists and editors formerly associated with the *Wall Street Journal*. In 2011, the Democrats hired Fusion GPS to conduct opposition research on GOP presidential candidate Mitt Romney. In August 2015, Planned Parenthood retained Fusion GPS to investigate the series of undercover videos produced by David Daleiden and Sandra Merritt from the Center for Medical Progress that allegedly showed Planned Parenthood officials negotiating to sell fetal tissue from abortions to medical researchers. While a grand jury failed to indict Planned Parenthood officials, Darden and Merritt faced criminal felony charges in San Francisco for filming without permission and invading privacy.

Trump became the presumptive GOP presidential nominee on May 3, 2016, when he decisively won the GOP primary in Indiana and Senator Ted Cruz dropped out of the race. With Trump having secured enough delegates to win the GOP nomination on the first ballot at the Republican national nominating convention, Singer quit funding Fusion GPS. The GPS report on Trump up until that point had been relatively benign, and Singer became a strong supporter and donor to Trump's presidential campaign.

On April 26, 2016, Hillary Clinton's presidential campaign and the Democratic National Committee authorized Marc Elias, a partner in the Seattle-based Perkins Coie law firm and the lawyer of record for both Hillary's presidential campaign and the DNC, to retain Fusion GPS to complete the opposition on Trump.[11] Hillary's campaign paid Perkins Coie $5.6 million in legal fees from June 2015 through December 2016, while the DNC paid the law firm $3.6 million in "legal and compliance counseling" since 2015, though the *Washington Post* reported it was impossible to tell precisely how much of those sums were paid to Fusion GPS.[12] On November 1, 2017, Reuters reported that Perkins Coie had paid $1.02 million to Fusion GPS, of which Fusion GPS paid Orbis Business Intelligence, the company that hired Christopher Steele, a British MI6 intelligence officer with close ties to US intelligence, to compile the dossier. By July 2016, Steele delivered a copy of his "Russia dossier" on Trump to unnamed FBI counterintelligence officers and allegedly to British intelligence officers as well.

When President Obama released his "long-form birth certificate" in a White House press conference on April 27, 2011, Perkins Coie partner Judith Corley was identified as the person who had traveled to Hawaii to pick up the birth certificate from Loretta Fuddy, then the director of the Hawaii Department of Health. At that time, Corley was working as an attorney in the office of White House counsel and was responsible for representing President Obama in personal matters, a job she had assumed the previous year when Robert Bauer, a partner at Perkins Coie, left that job to become White House counsel.[13] Bauer is married to Anita Dunn, a political operative who established a reputation in 2009 for attacking Fox News for being "an arm of the GOP," an attack she launched from her position at the time as President Obama's White House communication director.[14] Since April 2016, former president Obama's official campaign organization, Organizing for America (OFA), has paid more than $972,000 to Perkins Coie, according to Federal Election Commission records.[15]

From June through June 2016, efforts by Fusion GPS to get US newspapers interested in publishing the "Russia dossier" failed when the newspapers were unable to verify the information. Finally, on October 31, 2016, approximately one week before the November 8 presidential election, *Mother Jones* was the first to break the news the "Russia dossier" existed, publishing an explosive article titled "A Veteran Spy Has Given the FBI Information Alleging a Russian Operation to Cultivate Donald Trump."[16]

By the end of October 2016, the FBI arranged to pay Steele to continue gathering intelligence on Donald Trump and Russia. However, the FBI canceled this payment after it became known that Steele had falsified the information in the "Russia dossier," and Fusion GPS increasingly became the subject of news stories and congressional inquiries, with President Trump decrying the "Russia dossier" as "fake news."[17]

As late as October 30, 2016, just 10 days before the election, Senate Minority Leader Harry Reid wrote a letter to then FBI director James Comey urging Comey to make the Fusion GPS "Russia dossier" public. "In my communications with you and other top officials in the national security community, it has become clear that you possess explosive information about close ties and coordination between Donald Trump, his top advisors, and the Russian government—a foreign interest openly hostile to the United States, which Trump praises at every opportunity," Reid wrote. "The public has a right to know this information. I wrote to you months ago calling for this information to be released to the public. There is no danger to American interests from releasing it. And yet, you continue to resist calls to inform the public of this critical information."[18]

Senator John McCain claimed that he first learned about the "Russia dossier" when attending the annual Halifax International Security Forum in Canada on November 18, 2016. According to the story McCain first told, he subsequently dispatched an emissary on a transatlantic flight to an undisclosed airport, where the emissary was handed the dossier. What has developed since then is the suggestion that Fusion GPS executives gave McCain a copy of the dossier once McCain agreed he would help disseminate it to the press.

On December 9, 2016, according to McCain's official story, McCain arranged a private meeting with then FBI director James Comey to hand over the dossier. On January 10, 2017, 10 days before Trump's Inauguration Day, BuzzFeed published an unredacted version of the document on its website. In an article titled "These Reports Allege Trump Has Deep Ties to Russia," BuzzFeed reported the unverified dossier contained allegations that the Russian government had been "cultivating, supporting, and assisting" then president-elect Donald Trump for years.[19]

The Deep State and Mainstream Media Peddle Fusion GPS "Fake News" as Truth

The day after BuzzFeed published what became known as Steele's "Golden Shower" dossier, President Trump tweeted, "Are we living in Nazi Germany?" The dossier, published anonymously, alleged video-recorded sexual improprieties with Russian prostitutes in Russia by Trump that were being used by the Kremlin to blackmail him as well as a sustained relationship between Russian intelligence and the Trump organization. "A failing pile of garbage," Trump blasted BuzzFeed for publishing the controversial dossier.[20]

News reports were touting that the dossier's author, Christopher Steele, was a respected intelligence agency veteran who ran the Russian desk at MI6 and possessed "deep knowledge of Russia and street skills in Moscow." It was printed widely that

McCain had turned the dossier over to Comey after consulting "with a senior British diplomat who knew and vouched for the dossier's author."[21]

Yet in the beginning of October 2017, approximately three weeks before the cover-up coordinated by the Clinton campaign and the DNC fell apart, the Deep State and the Hillary-supporting partisan mainstream media were still peddling the Fusion GPS "Russia dossier" as gospel truth. Mainstream media reporters insisted that Steele's dossier added support to a report released by the director of national intelligence on January 6, 2017, which reported that the FBI, CIA, and NSA all had "high confidence" in concluding that (1) Russian president Vladimir Putin ordered an influence campaign in 2016 aimed at the US presidential election; (2) Russia's goals were to undermine public faith in the US democratic process, denigrate Secretary Clinton, and harm her electability and potential presidency; and (3) Putin and the Russian government developed a clear preference for president-elect Trump.[22]

As late as October 7, 2017, the *Guardian* in London reported that the Trump-Russia dossier was "growing more significant" by the day and "casting an ever darker" shadow over President Trump. "Nine months after its first appearance, the set of intelligence reports known as the Steele dossier, one of the most explosive documents in modern political history, is still hanging over Washington, casting a shadow over the Trump administration that has only grown darker as time has gone by," the *Guardian* wrote. "The Senate and House intelligence committees are, meanwhile, asking to see Steele to make up their own mind about his findings. The ranking Democrat on the House committee, Adam Schiff, said that the dossier was 'a very important and useful guide to help us figure out what we need to look into.' The fact that Steele's reports are being taken seriously after lengthy scrutiny by federal and congressional investigators has far-reaching implications."[23]

Then on October 24, 2017, the *Washington Post* broke the story, and Perkins Coie confirmed the truth in a letter that the *Post* published: Hillary Clinton had covered up her role in paying for Steele's fraudulent dossier.[24] Fully one year after the controversy broke, the Clinton campaign and DNC had still not admitted that they ended up spending possibly as much as $9 million to have the now-discredited Fusion GPS "Russia dossier" attacking Trump with sexual indiscretions in Russia—as well as allegations that Trump colluded with Russian intelligence agents to defeat Clinton—written and publicized.

On October 24, 2017, White House Press Secretary Sarah Sanders tweeted, "The real Russia scandal? Clinton campaign paid for the fake Russia dossier, then lied about it & covered it up." Senate Judiciary Committee Chairman Chuck Grassley summed up the Fusion GPS affair as follows: "The idea that the FBI and associates of the Clinton campaign would pay Mr. Steele to investigate the Republican nominee for president in the run-up to the election raises . . . questions about the FBI's independence from politics, as well as the Obama administration's use of law enforcement and intelligence agencies for political ends."[25]

What came crashing down with the fraudulent Steele dossier was the narrative first developed by Hillary Clinton and then parroted by the partisan Clinton-loving mainstream media—namely, that Trump somehow rigged the election against Hillary by colluding with the Russians. In the background, what also came into question was the Clinton narrative that Trump was somehow responsible for the Russian hack that led to WikiLeaks publishing the DNC and John Podesta emails that had proven to be so destructive to Hillary's 2016 electoral hopes. If Trump had not colluded with Russia to steal the DNC and Podesta emails, purloin them to WikiLeaks, and have them published on the internet, then what possibly could Russia have done to help Trump win?

The only other anemic charge was that Russian-linked ads costing about $100,000 in total targeted Michigan and Wisconsin, two states critical to Trump's 2016 electoral victory. Even the most partisan in the mainstream media found it not credible to advance this claim when Hillary's campaign had spent in excess of $1 billion to get her elected. Step by step, even the most diehard of Clinton's supporters were being forced to admit the truth: Hillary Clinton lost the 2016 presidential campaign because she was a terrible candidate with a message of hard-left identity politics that the American people did not buy, except maybe in California, New York, and the Democratic-controlled minority-populated urban areas.

The Seth Rich Murder Case

WikiLeaks began publishing the Podesta emails on October 7, 2016, almost simultaneously with the *Washington Post* publishing the *Access Hollywood* video with Trump making lewd comments to Billy Bush—a coincidence that Trump accusers argued was further proof of Trump's collusion with Russia and WikiLeaks.[26] WikiLeaks continued publishing a total of 57,375 Podesta emails in a series of drops, with the final "Part 35" published on Election Day, November 7, 2016. The Democrats continued to claim based on the CrowdStrike study conducted for the DNC that the Russians had used Guccifer 2.0 to hack Podesta's emails. "We are not going to confirm the authenticity of stolen documents released by Julian Assange who has made no secret of his desire to damage Hillary Clinton," Clinton spokesman Glen Caplin told the press on October 7, 2016. "Guccifer 2.0 has already proven the warnings of top national security officials that documents can be faked as part of a sophisticated Russian misinformation campaign," Caplin continued.[27]

Despite desperate efforts to prove that Guccifer 2.0 was Russian, Guccifer 2.0's identity has remained undisclosed. The Democrats never succeeded in proving either that Guccifer 2.0 was Russian or that Guccifer 2.0 was responsible for stealing the DNC and Podesta emails that WikiLeaks published. To the contrary, Julian Assange has repeatedly suggested that the emails were leaked by Seth Rich, a DNC employee and supporter of Bernie Sanders who was fatally shot in the Bloomingdale neighborhood of Washington, DC, on the night of July 10, 2016, in what has remained an unsolved murder case.

In an interview broadcast on Dutch television on August 9, 2016, the host Eelco van Rosenthal asked Assange, "The stuff that you're sitting on, is an October Surprise in there?"

Assange insisted, "WikiLeaks never sits on material," even though he had previously said that WikiLeaks had more material related to the Hillary Clinton campaign that had yet to be published. Then on his own initiative, without being specifically asked, Assange began talking about Seth Rich. "Whistleblowers go to significant efforts to get us material—and often very significant risks," he volunteered. "There's a 27-year-old that works for the DNC who was shot in the back, murdered, just a few weeks ago, for unknown reasons, as he was walking down the streets in Washington."

Van Rosenthal objected and said that the murder of DNC staffer Seth Rich was a robbery.

"No, there's no findings," Assange answered.

"What are you suggesting?" van Rosenthal asked.

"I'm suggesting that our sources take risks, and they become concerned to see things occurring like that," Assange responded.[28]

There was no reason for Assange to have spontaneously brought up Seth Rich in the context of the risks his leakers take if Rich were not the leaker involved in the DNC and Podesta emails that WikiLeaks published.

On August 9, 2016, WikiLeaks offered a $20,000 reward "for information leading to the conviction for the murder of DNC staffer Seth Rich." Again, why would WikiLeaks do this if Seth Rich were not the leaker in question? Repeatedly, Assange has denied that the Russians "or any state party" supplied WikiLeaks with the DNC and/or Podesta emails.[29]

Cyber Experts Conclude WikiLeaks Emails an Inside Job, Not a Russian Hack

Perhaps the most convincing evidence that the Russians were not involved was published by the left-leaning *Nation* in an article in which former NSA experts concluded that the WikiLeaks emails resulted not from an outside hacking attack but as the result of a leak—an inside job by someone who had access to the DNC computer system.[30]

A memo prepared by the Veteran Intelligence Professionals for Sanity (VIPS), based on their own investigation, concluded that the theft of DNC emails was not a hack but "some kind of inside leak that did not involve Russia." VIPS, formed in 2003 by a group of former US intelligence officers with decades of experience working within the CIA, FBI, and NSA, conducted a technical analysis of the metadata from the Guccifer 2.0 intrusion into the DNC server on July 5, 2016, concluding, "The DNC data was copied onto a storage device that far exceeds an Internet capability for a remote hack." The report also noted, "The forensics show that the copying was performed on the East coast of the United States."[31]

VIPS asked President Obama to disclose any evidence that WikiLeaks received DNC data from the Russians. VIPS noted that President Obama, at a press conference on January 18, 2017, described the conclusions of the intelligence community as "not conclusive," even though the intelligence community assessment of January 6, 2017, had expressed "high confidence" that Russian intelligence had relayed material it acquired from the DNC to WikiLeaks.

"Obama's admission came as no surprise to us," the VIPS report concluded. "It has long been clear to us that the reason the U.S. government lacks conclusive evidence of a transfer of a 'Russian hack' to WikiLeaks is because there was no such transfer. Based mostly on the cumulatively unique technical experience

of our ex-NSA colleagues, we have been saying for almost a year
that the DNC data reached WikiLeaks via a copy/leak by a DNC
insider."

FBI Reliance on Discredited Fusion GPS "Russia Dossier" Could Threaten Manafort Prosecution

Approximately half of the attorneys hired by Special Counselor
Robert Mueller were found to have contributed to the campaigns
of either Hillary Clinton or Barack Obama.[32] The bias toward
hiring pro-Clinton attorneys lends credence to the charge that
Mueller had set out to conduct a one-sided partisan investigation
into allegations that the Trump campaign colluded with Russia
while ignoring the evidence discussed in the next chapter, including Secretary Clinton's Uranium One scandal, the Democrats'
involvement financing and promoting the discredited Fusion
GPS "Russia dossier," and the continued allegations that the
Clinton Foundation since inception has been a vast, criminal
conspiracy with extensive ties to Russia. The political bias demonstrated in Mueller's hiring of staff attorneys prompted President Trump to question Mueller's integrity. "I can say that the
people that have been hire[d] are all Clinton supporters," Trump
alleged in a clip that was aired by Fox News's *Fox & Friends* in June
2017.[33]

On September 19, 2017, CNN reported that US investigators
electronically surveilled Manafort both before and after the election under a Foreign Intelligence Surveillance Court warrant.[34]
The CNN article cited only unnamed sources, strongly suggesting that the information was based on an illegal leak to the press
that could end up being traced back to the FBI, to Mueller's special counselor office, or to both. CNN reported that the secret
FISA warrant was obtained after Manafort became the subject
of the FBI investigation that began as early as 2014 under then
FBI director James Comey and centered on work Manafort conducted while consulting with Ukraine. "Some of the intelligence

collected includes communications that sparked concerns among investigators that Manafort had encouraged the Russians to help with the campaign, according to three sources familiar with the investigation," CNN reported. "Two of these sources, however, cautioned that the evidence is not conclusive."

On October 30, 2017, Mueller charged Manafort for laundering money related to financial transactions with Ukraine in the years 2006–7 without any proof that these alleged financial crimes were in any way linked to Trump campaign collusion with Russia to interfere in the 2016 election. Mueller's indictment said nothing about Trump campaign collusion with Russia, focusing instead on charging Manafort with criminal money laundering and tax evasion involving the work he did in Ukraine, work he had discontinued two years before he joined Trump as campaign manager.

What is not known for certain is whether Mueller used the Fusion GPS dossier to obtain Foreign Intelligence Surveillance Court surveillance. At a House Judiciary Committee hearing on December 7, 2017, the FBI director refused to answer direct questions from Representative Jim Jordan (Republican, Ohio) as to whether the Fusion GPS dossier had been used by the FBI to obtain court approval to conduct electronic surveillance against members of Donald Trump's presidential campaign.[35]

Under the "fruit of the poisonous tree" doctrine established by the Supreme Court in Fourth Amendment illegal search-and-seizure cases, the FBI and/or Mueller may have compromised their entire investigation of Trump campaign officials, including Manafort, by using either the fraudulent Fusion GPS dossier or information derived from it to obtain Foreign Intelligence Surveillance Court–authorized electronic surveillance.

CHAPTER 8

The Truth about "Russian Collusion"

Of the 28 US, European and Russian companies that participated in Skolkovo, 17 of them were Clinton Foundation donors.

—Peter Schweizer, *The New York Post*, July 2016

THE TRUTH ABOUT "RUSSIAN collusion" begins with the complex saga of Uranium One, a company created by Canadian entrepreneur Frank Giustra in conjunction with the assistance of former president Bill Clinton. The story begins in 2004–5, when Giustra and Clinton decided to corner the uranium market in Kazakhstan, and ends with the Clinton Foundation receiving $500,000 for a speech Bill Clinton gave in Moscow. The speaking fee was paid by Renaissance Capital (RenCap), a Cyprus-registered corporation controlled by former Russian intelligence officers with close ties to Russian president Vladimir Putin. After all was said and done, Russia gained control of 20 percent of all US uranium production with the blessings of Secretary of State Hillary Clinton and the Obama administration.

What this chapter will demonstrate is that while US investigators have failed to find any evidence that the Trump campaign colluded with Russia to defeat Clinton in 2016, there is extensive evidence that the real Russian collusion involved Democrats. Yet the Deep State continues to control the mainstream media narrative. So far, the Clintons and the Democrats have avoided FBI and DOJ scrutiny for their "Russian collusion" while Special Counselor Mueller continues his investigation with leaks, suggesting his goal is to develop criminal charges against President Trump.

Curing HIV/AIDS in Kazakhstan

In 2004, Canadian Frank Giustra, who started his career as a penny-stock dealer in Vancouver, British Columbia, attracted investors to put together a company that was eventually called

UrAsia Energy Ltd. The Clinton-Giustra tag-team effort to reap riches from uranium began on September 6, 2005, when Bill Clinton claimed that he and Frank Giustra just happened to be in Almaty, Kazakhstan, on the same day.

Clinton supposedly was there to announce a Clinton Foundation agreement enabling the government to buy low-cost HIV drugs. This story lacks credibility when we realize that the HIV problem in Kazakhstan at that time was virtually nonexistent (only 1,500 cases reported), and the generic drugs the Clintons were peddling were found ultimately to be defectively manufactured by the Indian drug company Ranbaxy, and as such, ineffective in combating the disease. Bill Clinton's desire to cure AIDS/HIV in Kazakhstan was an obvious pretext when we appreciate that Kazakhstan, the Central Asian country that was once part of the former Soviet Union, possesses some 12 percent of the world's uranium resources. With Kazakhstan's expanding mining capabilities, the country became the leading uranium producer in 2009, accounting for 28 percent of world uranium production, a percentage that has grown to 39 percent in 2015–16.[1]

Meanwhile, Giustra wanted to see if he could talk his way into an ownership interest in several uranium mines. Giustra got Kazakhstan's ruling despot at the time, Nursultan Nazarbayev—identified as a "torturer and human-rights violator"—to approve the coveted uranium deal for UrAsia, even though UrAsia was a start-up company with virtually no experience in the highly competitive uranium business.[2] Moukhtar Dzhakishev, president of Kazatomprom, the government agency that runs Kazakhstan's uranium mines and nuclear energy industry, has subsequently revealed that then senator Hillary Clinton pressured Kazakh officials to cede the uranium rights to Giustra that he requested.

The *New York Times* reported that once the 2005 uranium agreement with Kazakhstan was final, the next year, Giustra donated $31.3 million to the Clinton Foundation to help fight HIV/AIDS in Africa as a payoff, a gift that remained secret until one month before the *Times* published its exposé in 2008. "The gift, combined with Mr. Giustra's more recent and public pledge to give the William J. Clinton Foundation an additional $100 million, secured Mr. Giustra a place in Mr. Clinton's inner circle, an exclusive club of wealthy entrepreneurs in which friendship with the former president has its privileges," reporters noted.[3]

All this suggests that Bill Clinton and Frank Giustra arriving in Kazakhstan on the same day in 2005 was not coincidental.

Russia Deploys Spies to the United States to Bribe Clintons

Andrew C. McCarthy, the columnist for the *National Review* who previously served as an assistant US attorney for the Southern District of New York, has argued that Russia was outraged that Kazakhstan, formerly a part of the Soviet Union, had allowed Bill Clinton and Frank Giustra to walk off with the lucrative uranium contract.[4] In May 2009, Russia arrested Dzhakishev, president of Kazatomprom, and charged him with stealing uranium assets and embezzling shares in uranium mines as well as money laundering and bribe taking. In March 2010, Dzhakishev was convicted to 14 years in a maximum-security prison. The *Financial Times* in London noted that under Dzhakishev's leadership, Kazatomprom was transformed from "a bankrupt Soviet mining behemoth into a global nuclear power company with partners in North America, Europe, Japan, China, and Russia."[5] But Dzhakishev's mistake was allowing Clinton and Giustra to grab Kazakh uranium mines that Putin coveted.

Putin ultimately resolved that his best approach to solve the problem was to have the Russian government–controlled energy company Rosatom acquire Uranium One, thereby recapturing the interests in Kazakhstan uranium mines that Uranium One had managed to acquire.[6] To implement this plan, Putin decided to launch an espionage operation in the United States with the goal of bribing the Clintons to allow Rosatom to acquire

Uranium One. To implement his scheme, Putin used the Kremlin-controlled trucking company Tenex (a subsidiary of Rosatom). In 1992, President George H. W. Bush had allowed Tenex to operate in the United States to transfer uranium purchased from Russia's dissembled nuclear warheads to the United States after the uranium had been down-blended from its highly enriched weapons-grade level. Tenex operated in the United States through Tenam USA, a company operating in Bethesda, Maryland, that was run by Vadim Mikerin, a Russian official from Rosatom.

In arranging contracts with Tenam/Rosatom with US companies purchasing Russian uranium, Mikerin engaged in a scheme of defrauding the US contractors into paying inflated prices for uranium, with the excess proceeds laundered through shell companies and secret bank accounts in Latvia, Cyprus, Switzerland, and the Seychelles Islands. "The inflated payments served two purposes: They enriched Kremlin-connected energy officials in the U.S. and in Russia to the tune of millions of dollars; and they compromised the American companies that paid the bribes, rendering players in U.S. nuclear energy—a sector critical to national security—vulnerable to blackmail by Moscow," former prosecutor Andrew McCarthy noted.[7]

In 2009, to further Putin's scheme of acquiring Uranium One, Mikerin hired as a "lobbyist" or "consultant" an associate connected to Russian organized-crime groups who was to implement the strategy of Uranium One bribing its way to an increasing control of the US uranium market. Uncomfortable that Mikerin's extortion scheme that involved Russian suitcases stuffed with $100 bills was criminal, the lobbyist went to the FBI to expose the wrongdoing. Rather than prosecute the lobbyist, the FBI recruited the lobbyist to participate in the Russian racketeering scheme as "a confidential source," identified only as "CS-1" in government affidavits.

FBI investigation into the Tenam/Rosatom extortion and bribery scheme was based out of Maryland, where then FBI director

Robert Mueller put the investigation under the control of Rod J. Rosenstein, then US attorney in Maryland. Recall that when Attorney General Jeff Sessions recused himself from the "Russian collusion" investigation, Rosenstein acting as deputy attorney general appointed his former boss, Robert Mueller, to serve as the special counselor investigating Trump.

With the assistance of CS-1, the FBI made secret recordings and intercepted emails as early as 2009 that showed the Moscow-compromised uranium trucking company Tenam engaged in a racketeering scheme of bribes and kickbacks in violation of the Foreign Corrupt Practices Act. This was occurring while Russian nuclear officials routed millions of dollars to the United States to benefit the Clinton Foundation and while Secretary Clinton served on the Committee on Foreign Investment in the United States (CFIUS).

CFIUS is the interagency committee operating out of the Treasury that would have to vote to give Rosatom permission to acquire ownership interests in Uranium One. Note that CFIUS voted twice, first in 2010 and finally in 2013, to approve Rosatom's acquisition of Uranium One, without being told that the FBI had been investigating the Russians since 2009 for operating a spy network through Tenam USA with the goal of bribing their way into getting CFIUS approval for Rosatom to acquire Uranium One. "The Russians were compromising American contractors in the nuclear industry with kickbacks and extortion threats, all of which raised legitimate security concerns," noted investigative reporters John Solomon and Alison Spann, quoting an informant in an article published by the *Hill* on October 17, 2017—the article that first broke the news the Obama FBI had suppressed the Russian spy/bribery racketeering scheme.[8]

The involvement of Rosenstein and Mueller in suppressing the Russian bribery scheme should be sufficient evidence to disqualify both from investigating President Trump. Clearly, Rosenstein and Mueller understood that CFIUS would never have granted

permission for Rosatom to buy Uranium One if the Russian bribery scheme had been fully disclosed to the public in 2010. If the
DOJ opens an investigation into the Uranium One case, Mueller
will almost certainly find himself the subject of hard scrutiny. As
a target of a DOJ criminal investigation, the pressure on Mueller
to step down as special counselor in the Russian collusion investigation targeting the Trump campaign will be intense.

This case highlights yet again the degree to which Mueller and
Rosenstein function within the federal justice system as Deep
State operatives. The Uranium One case should be added to the
long list of cases in which Mueller, Comey, Holder, and Lynch
have conspired to end investigations that could well have produced criminal charges against Bill and Hillary Clinton as well
as Barack Obama. The corruption of the FBI and DOJ clearly
impacted the 2016 elections, as "Drain the swamp!" and "Lock
her up!" were chanted by Trump supporters at virtually every
campaign rally Trump held on his way to being elected president.

Russia Takes Control of Uranium One

A State Department memorandum dated June 28, 2009, released
by WikiLeaks, documented that on June 15, 2009, Uranium One
bought a 50 percent stake in a high-value Kazakhstan uranium
holding company, of which Kazakhstan's state nuclear company Kazatomprom owned the other 50 percent.[9] In October
2010, CFIUS voted to allow Rosatom to acquire majority control
(51 percent) of Uranium One. At that time, Secretary Clinton
and Attorney Eric Holder were members of the committee, with
Obama administration Treasury Secretary Timothy Geithner
serving as chairman.

Although Hillary Clinton denies that she was personally
involved and did not vote, records show that Hillary was in close
contact with Jose Fernandez, the person who cast the proxy vote
for Hillary as the State Department representative on CFIUS
when the Rosatom vote was taken. Fernandez pledged his loyalty

to Clinton in return for an assurance from John Podesta that he would receive a position on the board of Podesta's leftist Center for American Progress.[10]

In 2013, through its subsidiary, ARMZ Uranium Holding, Russian state-owned Rosatom acquired 100 percent of Uranium One in a transaction valued at $1.3 billion.[11] That same year, CFIUS voted a second time to approve the deal, giving official US government blessing to the Russians owning Uranium One, a transaction that allowed the Russian government to control one-fifth of all uranium production capacity in the United States.

According to a *New York Times* article, between 2008 and 2010, Uranium One and UrAsia investors gave $8.66 million in donations to the Clinton Foundation.[12] By the time the Russians had acquired 100 percent of Uranium One in 2013, nine of the shareholders in the company had reportedly contributed $145 million in donations to the foundation.[13]

Throughout the 2010–13 period, FBI Director Robert Mueller (who served as the head of the FBI from September 4, 2001, to September 4, 2013) did nothing to investigate the complex payments to the Clinton Foundation that give the appearance of a "pay-to-play" arrangement with Frank Giustra that allowed the Clintons to reap millions of dollars, provided Secretary of State Hillary Clinton did her part to guarantee CFIUS approval of the Uranium One deal with Putin's Rosatom.

A linchpin of the Clinton argument that the Uranium One deal had been investigated multiple times and there was nothing new to find was that Uranium One had been prohibited by the Nuclear Regulatory Commission (NRC) from shipping any US uranium overseas.

On November 2, 2017, investigative reporters John Solomon and Alison Spann printed a story in the *Hill* revealing that NRC memos received by the publication show that the commission did approve the shipment of yellowcake uranium, the uranium used to make nuclear fuel and weapons, from the Russian-owned mines in the United States to Canada in 2012 through a third party.[14] Subsequently, the Obama administration approved some of that uranium to be shipped to Europe.

While the NRC insisted that these overseas shipments only lasted from 2012 to 2014, it is clear the commission authorized an amendment to an existing export license for a Kentucky-based trucking firm called RSB Logistics Services Inc. to add Uranium One to the list of clients whose uranium it could move to Canada. The investigative reporters noted that these arrangements were hidden from Congress, leaving open the question of whether the Russian bribery scheme could have created other third-party shipment arrangements that would have circumvented the NRC reassurances that the Uranium One deal could not possibly result in a shipment of US yellowcake uranium ending up in the hands of the Russians.

So by getting CFIUS to allow Rosatom to acquire 100 percent of Uranium One in 2013, Putin achieved his goal of not only recapturing the Kazakhstan uranium rights that Bill Clinton and Frank Giustra had obtained in 2009 but also obtaining the right to transport Uranium One production overseas. "Fifteen months before the 13 members of the Committee on Foreign Investment in the United States, known as CFIUS, approved the sale of the Canadian Company Uranium One to Russia's nuclear arm giant Rosatom, the FBI began investigating persons who were connected to the Russian state corporation," investigative journalist Sara A. Carter wrote.[15] Carter noted that the FBI said in court and in interviews that by 2010, they had gathered enough evidence to prove that Rosatom-connected officials were engaged in a global bribery scheme that included kickbacks and money laundering. "FBI officials said the investigation could have prevented the sale of Uranium One, which controlled 20 percent of U.S. uranium supply under U.S. law," Carter stressed.

Mueller Delivers Uranium to Russia
on a Secret Mission for Hillary

On May 17, 2017, the day Deputy Attorney General Rod J. Rosenstein appointed former FBI director Robert Mueller as special counsel, Julian Assange tweeted a reference to a WikiLeaks-released State Department cable that documented Secretary of State Hillary Clinton ordering Mueller to deliver a sample of stolen highly enriched uranium (HEU) to Russia in 2009.

The WikiLeaks tweet referenced a Secretary of State Clinton sent to John Beyrle, US ambassador in Russia and the US ambassador to the embassy in Tbilisi, Georgia, and the Russian Embassy, dated August 17, 2009, indicating that FBI Director Mueller was planning to fly to Moscow on September 21, 2009, to deliver a sample of highly enriched uranium (HEU) that the cable identified had been confiscated by the US Department of Energy during a 2006 "nuclear smuggling sting operation involving one Russian national and several Georgian accomplices."[16]

The key operational language of the cable was contained in paragraph six: "(S/Rel Russia) Action request: Embassy Moscow is requested to alert at the highest appropriate level the Russian Federation that FBI Director Mueller plans to deliver the HEU sample once he arrives to Moscow on September 21. Post is requested to convey information in paragraph 5 with regard to chain of custody, and to request details on Russian Federation's plan for picking up the material. Embassy is also requested to reconfirm the April 16 understanding from the FSB verbally that we will have no problem with the Russian Ministry of Aviation concerning Mueller's September 21 flight clearance."

On June 19, 2017, Shepard Ambellas, the editor in chief of Intellihub.com, noted that the classified State Department cable in question that proposed Director Mueller should be the one to personally conduct the transfer of a 10-gram sample of HEU to Russian law enforcement sources during a secret "plane-side" meeting on a "tarmac" in early fall of 2009 was reminiscent of "the infamous Loretta Lynch/Bill Clinton meeting which occurred on a Phoenix, Arizona, tarmac, back in June of 2016."[17]

Exactly why Secretary Clinton decided it was critical to arrange a clandestine transfer of this purloined uranium sample back to Russia, carried out by Director Mueller in a secret trip to Moscow, has never been made clear. However, several WikiLeaks cables show that the State Department had been tracking Uranium One dealings with Kazakhstan since 2008.[18]

While Clinton apologists have insisted that Mueller's secret mission to Russia has no connection to Uranium One or Secretary Clinton's role in the CFIUS votes that allowed Putin to control 20 percent of US uranium,[19] the issue demands detailed investigation, especially because there is abundant evidence that Mueller turned a blind eye to numerous highly suspicious, potentially criminal Uranium One transactions related to Frank Giustra.

On January 26, 2007, the Associated Press reported that Igor Shkabura, deputy director of the Bochvar Inorganic Materials Unit, said the sample of uranium seized in the sting operation was weapons grade, but the sample was too small to determine its origin, according to reports published by Russian news agencies RIA-Novosti and ITAR-Tass.

Given that Russia already had samples of the HEU stolen in 2006, what value was there to the very small 10-gram amount the United States possessed that would justify Director Mueller personally conducting a clandestine mission to make a tarmac drop of the US sample in Moscow? Exactly why Secretary of State Hillary Clinton ordered FBI Director Robert Mueller to make a secret trip to Russia remains shrouded in mystery.

Podesta Group, DC Lobbyist for Russian Bank Accused in Ukraine of Terrorist Ties

While the mainstream media continues to obsess over Paul Manafort and General Michael Flynn's supposed "Russian collusion," totally ignored are the ties Tony Podesta, the brother of Hillary's 2016 presidential campaign chairman, John Podesta, had to both Uranium One and Sberbank, Moscow's largest state-run bank, which has close ties to international terrorism and Russian president Vladimir Putin.

As the Russians gained control of Uranium One from 2009 through 2013, the Podesta Group was paid a total of $630,000 between 2010 and 2015 to represent Uranium One, the Russian-controlled firm with close financial ties to the Clinton Foundation that today controls 20 percent of all US uranium produced.[20]

Among the revelations made public through the 11.5 million documents leaked by the International Consortium of Investigative Journalists detailing the legal and financial arrangements behind secretive offshore banking transactions dating back to the 1970s was the disclosure that Sberbank uses the Podesta Group as its registered lobbyist in Washington.

"Sberbank (Savings Bank in Russian) engaged the Podesta Group to help its public image—leading Moscow financial institutions not exactly being known for their propriety and wholesomeness—and specifically to help lift some of the pain of sanctions placed on Russia in the aftermath of the Kremlin's aggression against Ukraine, which has caused real pain to the country's hard-hit financial sector," wrote former National Security Agency analyst and counterintelligence officer John R. Schindler in an article titled "Panama Papers Reveal Clinton's Kremlin Connection" published by the *Observer* on April 7, 2016. "It's hardly surprising that Sberbank sought the help of Democratic insiders like the Podesta Group to aid them in this difficult hour, since they clearly understand how American politics work," he continued. "The question is why the Podesta Group took Sberbank's money," Schindler asked. "That financial institution isn't exactly hiding in the shadows—it's the biggest bank in Russia, and its reputation leaves a lot to be desired. Nobody acquainted with Russian finance was surprised that Sberbank wound up in the Panama Papers."[21]

Schindler noted that since the 1990s, Sberbank has grown to be Russia's dominant bank, controlling nearly 30 percent of Russia's aggregate banking assets and employing a quarter of a million people. The majority stockholder in Sberbank is Russia's Central Bank, making Sberbank functionally an arm of the Russian government, though officially, Sberbank is a private institution. "Certainly, Western intelligence is well acquainted with Sberbank, noting its close relationship with Vladimir Putin and his regime. Funds moving through Sberbank are regularly used to support clandestine Russian intelligence operations, while the bank uses its offices abroad as cover for the Russian Foreign Intelligence Service or SVR," Schindler pointed out.[22]

A NATO counterintelligence official explained that Sberbank, which has outposts in almost two dozen foreign countries, "functions as a sort of arm of the SVR outside Russia, especially because many of its senior employees are 'former' Russian intelligence officers." Inside the country, Sberbank has an equally cozy relationship with the Federal Security Service (FSB), Russia's powerful domestic intelligence agency.

On April 17, 2014, the *Moscow Times* reported that Ukraine opened criminal proceedings against Sberbank and 13 other banks on suspicion of "financing terrorism."[23] Schindler noted the Ukrainian criminal investigation had concluded that Sberbank had distributed millions of dollars in illegal aid to Russian-backed separatists fighting in Eastern Ukraine, with the bank serving as "a witting supporter of Russian aggression against Ukraine."

On April 5, 2016, Lachlan Markay, reporting in the *Washington Free Beacon*, published the lobbying registration form the Podesta Group filed with the US government, proving that Sberbank had contracted with the Podesta Group to advance their interests with banking, trade, and foreign relations.[24] According to the

Organized Crime and Corruption Reporting Project produced by
Panama Papers journalist, Sberbank has ties to companies used
by members of Putin's inner circle to funnel state resources into
lucrative private investments.[25]

On March 30, 2016, Politico reported that the Podesta Group
registered to lobby for the US subsidiary of Sberbank to see if
relief could be obtained for the bank in the easing of US sanctions against Russia for Russia's role in the Ukraine conflict.[26]

John Podesta Briefly Served as Clinton Foundation CEO

According to a *New York Times* report published August 13, 2013,
a wave of midlevel program staff members departed the Clinton
Foundation in 2011, "reflecting the frustration of much of the
foundation's policy personnel with the old political hands running the organization."[27]

Around that time, Bruce Lindsey, then the Clinton Foundation's CEO, suffered a stroke, underscoring concerns about the
foundation's line of succession. John Podesta, a chief of staff in
Mr. Clinton's White House, stepped in for several months as tem-
porary chief executive.

Hillary's "Russia Reset" and the Sale of Military Technology to Russia

According to information recently released in the Panama Papers,
John Podesta, Hilary Clinton's presidential campaign manager,
is implicated in the Clinton Foundation's shadowy offshore
money-laundering operations, receiving money from Russia
apparently in exchange for the transfer of US advanced technology, including technology with military implications, arranged
by Secretary of State Hillary Clinton as part of her "Russian reset"
strategy with Vladimir Putin.[28] During his 2009 visit to Moscow,
President Obama announced the creation of a US Russia Bilat-
eral Presidential Commission, with Secretary Clinton heading

the American side and Foreign Minister Sergey Lavrov representing the Russians.

To implement this agreement, Secretary Clinton launched her "Russian reset" initiative, and Putin established the Skolkovo Innovation Center west of Moscow as an area styled to be built as Russia's alternative to Silicon Valley, with the Kremlin committed to spending $5 billion over the next three years to fund it. To head Skolkovo, Putin appointed Viktor Vekselberg, one of Russia's wealthiest oligarchs, who had become a multibillionaire through controlling the Renova Group, a Russian conglomerate with extensive investments in mining, oil and natural gas, and telecommunications.

The stated goal of Secretary Clinton's "Russian reset" policy was to identify US technology transfers to Russia that would attract US financiers to invest together with the Russian state investment fund Rusnano—a technology investment fund Putin created in 2007 by relying totally on Russian government funding.[29] Dozens of US tech firms, including Clinton Foundation donors like Google, Intel, and Cisco, made major financial contributions to Skolkovo, with Cisco committing $1 billion. By 2012, the vice president of the Skolkovo Foundation, Conor Lenihan—the minister of state at Irish Aid who had participated with the Clinton Foundation, contributing €70 million in Irish government funds to fight HIV/AIDS in Africa[30]—reported that Skolkovo had assembled 28 Russian, American, and European "key partners," 17 of whom (60 percent) had made financial commitments totaling tens of millions of dollars to the Clinton Foundation or sponsored speeches by Bill Clinton.

State Department emails revealed that three months after Putin appointed Vekselberg to head the Skolkovo Project, a Clinton Foundation employee began pushing the State Department to approve a planned trip by Bill Clinton to Russia to meet with Vekselberg and a handful of other Russian investments.[31] Donor records show Vekselberg's Renova group had contributed between $50,000 and $100,000 to the Clinton Foundation, with another firm associated with Vekselberg, OC Oerlikon, donating $25,000 to the Clinton Foundation.

The US Army Foreign Military Studies program at Fort Leavenworth concluded in 2012 that the purpose of Skolkovo was to serve as a vehicle for worldwide transfer to Russia in the areas of information technology, biomedicine, energy, satellite and space technology, as well as nuclear technology. Soon the US government was aware that the Obama administration was approving the transfer of classified, sensitive, and emerging military technology to Russia, including approving the first weapons-related project in the development of a hypersonic cruise missile engine.

A 2006 report titled "From Russia with Money," released in August by the Government Accountability Institute—where "Clinton Cash" author Peter Schweizer is president and Steve Bannon, a key advisor to Donald Trump's campaign and White House, was a director—charged that Secretary Clinton used the "Russian reset" and the Skolkovo Project to funnel US military technology to Russia.[32]

Russia Pays Off Podesta in Complex International Money-Laundering Scheme

In June and July 2011, while he was advising Clinton on State Department policy, John Podesta joined the board of three related entities: Joule Unlimited, a small Massachusetts-based energy company; its holding company, Joule Global Holdings NV, which was based in the Netherlands; and Joule Global Stichting, which appears to be the ultimate controlling entity. In a complicated chain of connections familiar to those conversant with how international money-laundering transactions are structured, Viktor Vekselberg made a multi-million-dollar investment into Joule Unlimited, the small Massachusetts-based energy company, owned by Joule Global Holdings NV in the Netherlands.

The investment was laundered from Rusnano to Renova in a deal that made sense to Russian financial authorities given Vekselberg's role as president of the Skolkovo Foundation. The Government Accountability Institute report "From Russia with Money" noted that Russia created the Joule group of companies supposedly to develop technologies aimed at harnessing solar energy.

Although following international money-laundering trails is a complicated process, the key point is that two months after Podesta joined the Joule Unlimited board, Vladimir Putin's Rusnano announced that it would invest up to $35 million in Joule Unlimited. On August 1, 2016, Bannon and Schweizer coauthored an article in Breitbart titled "Report: Hillary Clinton's Campaign Manager John Podesta Sat on Board of Company That Bagged $35 Million from Putin-Connected Russian Government Fund."[33]

Podesta, it turns out, also consulted with the Wyss Foundation, a group controlled by Swiss billionaire Hansjörg Wyss, an investor in Joule Energy. Podesta was paid $87,000 by the Wyss Foundation in 2013 according to federal tax records. Wyss was also a major Clinton Foundation donor, with the Wyss Foundation contributing between $1 million and $5 million. To complete the circle, Vekselberg, the Renova Group, and the Skolkovo Foundation joined Wyss in establishing ties to the Clinton Foundation, either as substantial donors or as participants in the Clinton Global Initiative.

Bannon and Schweizer further reported that Podesta's far-left think tank, Center for American Progress (CAP), took in $5.25 million from the Sea Change Foundation between 2010 and 2013. The Sea Change Foundation, it turns out, ties into various entities specifically named and investigated in the Panama Papers, including Klein Ltd. and Troika Dialog Ltd.

Metcombank appears to be the bank Vekselberg has used to make transfers to the Clinton Foundation, with the money flowing from the Moscow branch of Metcombank to Deutsche Bank and Trust Company Americas, with the money finally ending up in a private bank account in the Bank of America in New York City that is operated by the Clinton Foundation.[34]

Here is what the Government Accountability Institute report had to say about the Sea Change Foundation: "Who was funding Sea Change Foundation? According to tax records, Sea Change Foundation at the time was receiving a large infusion of funds from a mysterious Bermuda-based entity called 'Klein, Ltd.' . . . Who owns Klein? It is impossible to say exactly, given corporate secrecy laws in Bermuda. But the registered agent and lawyers who set up the offshore entity are tied to a handful of Russian business entities including Troika Dialog, Ltd. Leadership includes Ruben Vardanyan, an ethnic Armenian who is a mega oligarch in Putin's Russia. Vardanyan also served on the board of Joule Energy with John Podesta."

"Why Hillary Clinton's State Department and her campaign manager were tied up in this raises serious questions that demand answers and transparency," Bannon and Schweizer concluded.

Podesta Payoff in Russian Money-Laundered Stock Options

In an email dated January 6, 2014, Mark Solakian, a senior vice president and general counsel with Joule Unlimited, emailed Podesta, confirming that Podesta had exercised 75,000 shares out of 100,000 options in Joule Unlimited that he had been issued in 2011 under stock option agreement issued to him in partial compensation for his work on the Joule board of directors.[35] Solakian confirmed that Podesta had transferred the resulting 75,000 common shares of Joule Unlimited common shares to Leonidio Holdings LLC in a transaction that most likely would prevent the 75,000 common shares of Joule stock from showing up directly as an asset owned in any financial statement Podesta prepared.

Leonidio Holdings LLC is a private company listed in Salt Lake City, Utah, that was subsequently transferred to the address of Podesta's daughter, Megan Rouse, at 7962 Shannon Court in

Dublin, California, where his daughter operates a financial planning company. By transferring ownership of the Joule stock to an account registered to his daughter, Podesta appears to have engaged in a process of asset structuring, whose purpose may have been to hide the asset from public disclosure and/or avoid certain tax consequences that may have resulted from public disclosure.

What is clear from the emails released by WikiLeaks is that Podesta confirmed that he transferred 25,146 shares of Series C preferred shares and 8,547 Series C-II preferred shares of Joule Unlimited stock to Leonidio Holdings LLC. The shares were subsequently transferred to the address of his daughter's company, Megan Rouse Financial Planning.

Same Ukrainian Group Contracting Manafort Also Contracted Podesta Group

Special Counselor Robert Muller, in his investigation into Tony Podesta, disclosed that the same Ukrainian group, the European Centre for a Modern Ukraine (ECMU), that established a public relations contract with Paul Manafort also established a similar contract with the Podesta Group.

On December 20, 2013, in a disclosure largely ignored by the mainstream media as the Manafort controversy developed after the 2016 election, Reuters reported that ECMU had paid $900,000 to the Podesta Group for a two-year contract aimed at improving the image of the Yanukovych government in the United States. The Podesta Group told Reuters they were implementing this plan through contacts with key congressional Democrats.[36] To date, the mainstream media has focused attention largely only on the contract that Manafort's K-Street firm, Davis, Manafort & Freedman, established with the ECMU, not the contract established by the Podesta Group.

On February 21, 2014, Russian leader Vladimir Putin helped then president Yanukovych flee violent protests seeking to oust him from office. Yanukovych flew out of Ukraine and traveled through Crimea to arrive in Russia, where he has remained, trying desperately to restore himself to power back home in Kiev.[37] The background of the controversy traces back to 2007, when Yanukovych's political party, Ukraine's Party of Regions, hired the ECMU to perform an "extreme makeover," repositioning the party from being perceived as a "haven for Donetsk-based mobsters and oligarchs" into that of a legitimate political party.[38]

In Manafort's case, opponents have failed to document that Manafort ever received some $12.7 million in some 22 previously undisclosed cash payments from Yanukovych's pro-Russian party, as supposedly documented by "black ledger" entries revealed by Ukraine's National Anti-Corruption Bureau.[39] Yet this "evidence" was sufficient for *New York Times* reporters to conclude that Manafort had hidden back-channel ties to Putin financed by under-the-table payments arranged via Ukraine.[40]

From there, the Democratic Party narrative charges that Manafort never registered as a foreign agent with the US Justice Department, which would only have been required if he was contracted with the Ukrainian government, not with a political party in Ukraine, and that Manafort transferred his close relationship with Putin (via Yanukovych) to the Trump campaign. It turns out that the Podesta Group filed disclosures with the Justice Department, but only after the work Manafort was doing for ECMU was reported in the press.[41]

The Democratic Party narrative continues to suggest that Manafort's close relationship to the Kremlin allowed him to position the Trump campaign to receive hacked emails that embarrassed the Clinton campaign by exposing the efforts Debbie Wasserman Schultz, as chairman of the DNC, took to rig the primaries for Hillary, to the distinct disadvantage of challenger, Senator Bernie Sanders. However, this entire story is thrown into disarray if the Podesta brothers, via the Podesta Group, have tighter and more easily documentable financial ties to Russia, involving far greater numbers than have ever been suggested tie Manafort to Russia via Ukraine.

CNN further reported on August 19, 2016, that the Podesta Group had issued a statement upholding that the firm has retained the boutique Washington-based law firm Caplin & Drysdale "to determine if we were misled by the Centre for a Modern Ukraine or any other individuals with potential ties to foreign governments or political parties." The Podesta Group statement issued to CNN continued, "When the Centre became a client, it certified in writing that 'none of the activities of the Centre are directly or indirectly supervised, directed, controlled, financed or subsidized in whole or in part by a government of a foreign country or a foreign political party.' We relied on that certification and advice from counsel in registering and reporting under the Lobbying Disclosure Act rather than the Foreign Agents Registration Act." The statement concluded with the following: "We will take whatever measures are necessary to address this situation based on Caplin & Drysdale's review, including possible legal action against the Centre."

CHAPTER 9

Mainstream Media Attack Trump

Protesting has become a profession now. . . .
They have every right to do that, don't get me
wrong. . . . [But] this has become a very paid,
"AstroTurf"-type movement.

—Sean Spicer, February 2017

THE HARD-LEFT'S MANIPULATION OF the mainstream media involves more than a shared ideological world view. Mirroring the hard-left, the mainstream media favors a statist view of politics that seeks to extend massive government regulation over every aspect of life, ranging from issues debated in cultural wars to all aspects of the economy and international trade. The hard-left and the Deep State share a concern to expand statist control of a multinational corporate "one world government" welfare state that controls people from a cradle-to-grave reality.

Editors at publications including the *New York Times*, the *Washington Post*, and increasingly the *Wall Street Journal* have been supporters of Democratic Party socialist domestic policies, coupled with globalist international "free trade" agreements and unlimited open-borders immigration couched as "global migration patterns," since at least the administration of Lyndon B. Johnson in the 1960s and possibly as far back as the administration of Franklin Delano Roosevelt, starting with the 1930s Depression.

But in recent years, seasoned hard-left political operators have stepped up their game to achieve a new goal, aided been by extensive funding from leftist millionaires and billionaires and supplemented by the generosity of left-leaning foundations. No longer is the hard-left satisfied with the mainstream media reporting a biased version of the news. Today the hard-left aims to discredit conservative and libertarian political opponents as "conspiracy theorists" and "right-wing extremists." Sensing ultimate victory, the hard-left has begun its final stage of morphing the United States into a totalitarian state that tolerates no dissent, no freedom of religion—unless "belief in God" is consistent with the LGBT agenda—and no deviance from the politically correct dictates of identity politics.

David Brock, a conservative LGBT advocate who switched sides to the hard-left, runs his Media Matters organization with a determination to silence conservative and libertarian critics across all forms of media, including radio, television, print, and now internet-based social media and blogs. The goal of groups like Media Matters today is to block conservative and libertarian reporters and pundits from mainstream media acceptance, thereby blocking public dissemination of their views. The brass-knuckle tactics Brock espouses must be taken seriously, given his mean-spirited defense of his current attack-dog posture.

As soon as Donald Trump won the 2016 presidential election, Brock came forth to declare to his financial backers how he intended to position Media Matters to take the lead in the movement to resist and obstruct Trump's ability to rule. Brock's goal today is to weaponize the mainstream media's liberal bias by supercharging traditional public relations tactics for influencing media with Saul Alinsky–like community organizing tactics designed to provoke and ultimately win a war waged to remove conservatives and libertarians from America once and for all.

David Brock's Media Matters Declares War on Trump

In a briefing book titled "Media Matters, the Top Watchdog against Fake News and Propaganda: Transforming the Media Landscape," which Brock published privately in January 2017 to solicit donors for what Brock termed the "Media Matters for America 2020 Plan," Brock asserts his intention to declare war on Trump's ability to rule. "The onslaught of well-funded right-wing media brings with it significant challenges," reads the first sentence of Brock's solicitation, picking up with Media Matters's "core mission of disarming right-wing misinformation, while leading the fight against the next generation of conservative disinformation."[1]

Brock was among the first to coin "conservative disinformation" as "fake news" in the attempt to launch a "meme," or "narrative," designed to target reporters, pundits, and news media that dare publish conservative views differing from the hard-left views reported uncritically by obviously left-biased cable news channels such as CNN and MSNBC.

In the "Competitive Analysis" section, Brock singles out the conservative Media Research Center, for applying an $18 million annual operating budget to the goal of working "closely with establishment right-wing media to reinforce the myth of a liberally biased media, push journalism to the right and propel disinformation." Next, Brock attacks the website Breitbart for having received "millions in funding from extremist billionaires close to the Trump administration" while providing "a nexus point for the so-called alt-right (the newest branding for white nationalism, anti-Semitism, and misogyny) to exploit vulnerabilities through the media landscape."

Note here that Brock is also creating a narrative—adding to the meme—that the "alt-right" (another term created by Brock and the hard-left to attack conservatives) are haters, characterized as "white nationalists, anti-Semites, and misogynists," the new labels Brock and his coconspirators on the hard-left intend to apply (along with the accusation of being "racists") to any reporter, commentator, pundit, or news agency that refuses to uncritically parrot a hard-left ideological interpretation of current events. In addition, Brock leaves no doubt that Google and Facebook are his coconspirators in advancing the "fake news" meme against conservative and libertarian news organizations on the internet.

In the "Top Outcomes" section of the briefing book for donors, Brock lays out his goals for the coming four years of the Trump administration as follows:

- Serial misinformers and right-wing propagandists inhabiting everything from social media to the highest levels of government will be exposed.
- Internet and social media platforms, like Google and Facebook, will no longer uncritically and without consequence host and enrich fake news sites and propagandists.
- Toxic alt-right social media-fueled harassment campaigns that silence dissent and poison our national discourse will be punished and halted.

On November 14, 2016, six days after Donald J. Trump was elected president, the *New York Times* reported that Google had announced a policy that would ban websites "that peddle fake news" from using its online advertising service. Hours later, Facebook updated the language in its Facebook Audience Network policy, amending it to specify that Facebook "will not display ads in sites that show misleading or legal content, to include fake news sites."[2]

On January 25, 2007, Recode.com reported that Google, since declaring the policy against "fake news," had banned 200 publishers from using its AdSense network, an ad placement service that automatically places text and display ads on participating sites based on audience characteristics. Recode.com further reported that Google declined to provide a listing of the banned sites.[3]

In his briefing book, Brock acknowledged that while Google was a relatively easy sale on "fake news," Facebook was a much harder sale, with Mark Zuckerberg calling "crazy" the notion that "fake news is a problem."

So what did Media Matters do?

"In November, we launched a campaign pressuring Facebook to: 1) acknowledge the problem of the proliferation of fake news on Facebook and its consequences for our democracy and 2) commit to taking action to fix the problem," the Media Matters briefing book declared. "As a result of our push for accountability,"

Brock was happy to report, Facebook was responsive to both requests.

Soros Muscled Glenn Beck from Fox News, Pat Buchanan from MSNBC, and Lou Dobbs from CNN

Activists like David Brock have learned from George Soros how to use economic clout to push prominent conservative and libertarian personalities off cable news—a strategy Soros began pursuing in advance of Barack Obama's 2012 reelection campaign.

Among the 2,500 documents hacked from George Soros's Open Society Foundation are documents that explicitly discuss the Open Society Foundation funding various organizations to run an activist campaign aimed at ousting Glenn Beck from Fox News, Pat Buchanan from MSNBC, and Lou Dobbs from CNN.

In a memorandum dated March 27, 2012, Bill Vandenberg, the head of Soros's Democracy Fund, discusses a two-year $600,000 grant to support Color of Change that was targeted to allow the organization to hold "media companies accountable for derogatory actions, including successful campaigns to oust Glenn Beck from the Fox Network and Pat Buchanan from MSNBC."[4] Many documents prepared for the Open Society foundation board describe Color of Change as the largest online political activist group representing African American issues, with more than 900,000 due-paying members. Color of Change defines its mission as moving "decision-makers in corporations and government to create a more human and less hostile world for Black people in America." The organization boasts on its website of "designing strategies powerful enough to fight racism and injustice—in politics and culture, in the work place and the economy, in criminal justice and community life, and wherever they exist—we are changing both the written and unwritten rules of society."[5]

Vandenberg confirmed what has been long suspected by conservatives and libertarians—namely, that Soros has utilized his money to pay leftist advocacy groups to launch aggressive attacks on advertisers to force commentators like Beck, Buchanan, and Dobbs off cable news channels.

In June 2011, when Glenn Beck was fired from his highly popular hour-long weekday show on Fox News, *Huffington Post* attributed the firing to "an aggressive campaign that caused up to 400 advertisers to drip their support of the show," although news sources at the time failed to identify Soros as the culprit behind the organized campaign to pressure advertisers to abandon Beck on Fox.[6] PBS host Bill Meyers later acknowledged that Beck had been fired by Fox News because Beck had refused to take the advice of senior executives to ease up on attacking Soros on air.

In February 2012, Politico reported that MSNBC had finally reached a decision to sever relations with Pat Buchanan permanently after 10 years, in which time Buchanan had regularly appeared on the cable news channel. His firing was supposedly over a controversy surrounding his book *Suicide of a Superpower: Will America Survive to 2025?*[7]

In a piece published in the *American Conservative* on February 16, 2012, titled "Blacklisted, but Not Beaten," Buchanan agreed that Color of Change began issuing calls for his firing almost as soon as the book was published, proclaiming that his book espouses a "white supremacist ideology," pointing to chapter 4, "The End of White America," as proof of that statement.[8] Buchanan defended the thesis of his 2012 book, arguing, "America is Balkanizing, breaking down along the lines of religion, race, ethnicity, culture, and ideology and that Western peoples are facing demographic death by century's end." He further commented that the modus operandi of "the thought police at Color of Change" is to brand "any writer who dares to venture outside the narrow corral in which they seek to confine debate" as racist.

In a statement published on the group's website, Color of Change boasts that starting in 2009, the group forced Glenn Beck off cable television, holding his advertisers and Fox News accountable for his dangerous drumbeat of racist misinformation. "Beck legitimized disproven, racist ideas about the role of Black people in society by integrating them into mainstream political conversations," the posting read. "White supremacists praised him for helping to make their ideas more respectable and widespread. And he did it with the support of hundreds of major corporations that advertised on his show. No one was fighting back effectively; our movement didn't have an answer to Glenn Beck."[9] Color of Change revealed that the decision to drive Beck off the air was made in July 2008, when Beck called President Obama a "racist" with a "deep-seated hatred for white people."

Here is how Color of Change described their economic campaign waged against Beck:

> Within days of Beck's attack on President Obama, tens of thousands of Color Of Change members were signing our petition to all of Beck's advertisers, channeling our outrage into meaningful and strategic leverage over Fox News. At the same time, behind the scenes, our staff initiated a dialogue with some of Beck's biggest advertisers, corporations including Walmart, CVS, Best Buy and Sprint. We conveyed to them the concerns of our members, and presented them with a clear choice: stop funding Beck, or become publicly associated with his racism and divisiveness. We partnered with Media Matters to track ads on Beck's show, and worked with organizations including CREDO Action, MoveOn and Jewish Funds for Justice to draw more people into the campaign and increase the pressure.
>
> Most companies moved quickly to pull their ads, once they understood the power of our members to hold them accountable. When a corporation refused, our members took action, flooding them with hundreds of phone calls, and spreading content and commentary on social media that linked their brand to Beck and his attacks on Black

people. Nearly every corporation we targeted pulled their ads. The victories snowballed, continuing for months.[10]

More than 285,000 people signed a Color of Change petition to Beck's advertisers, demanding that Beck be removed from Fox News.

In an Open Society Foundation summary of US Programs (USP) for the Soros-funded Democracy and Power Fund in 2011–12, a chart credits that Soros's funding of various Hispanic advocacy groups was responsible for forcing CNN to cancel Lou Dobb's hour-long television program *Lou Dobbs Tonight*. The chart entry lists the Soros-funded grantees involved as (1) Citizen Engagement Lab, the parent group for the African American advocacy group Color of Change and the Hispanic advocacy group Presenté; (2) New Organizing Institute; and (3) Voto Latino.

On November 11, 2009, when Lou Dobbs made a surprise announcement that he had decided to quit CNN, Roberto Lovato, cofounder of Presenté, said, "Our contention all along was that Lou Dobbs—who has a long history of spreading lies and conspiracy theories about immigrants and Latinos—does not belong on the most trusted name in news. We are thrilled that Dobbs no longer has the legitimate platform from which to incite fear and hate."[11]

When charges of sexual harassment and misconduct involving Fox News host Bill O'Reilly arose in March and April 2017, Media Matters organized a boycott of O'Reilly's sponsors while fanning the flames with mainstream media outlets. On April 1, 2017, the *New York Times* reported that O'Reilly and Fox News's parent company, 21st Century Fox, had paid out approximately $13 million over two decades to a total of five women who agreed not to pursue litigation or speak about their accusations against O'Reilly for sexually inappropriate conduct.[12] On April 4, 2014, Media Matters published a list of companies that had pulled advertising from airing during *The O'Reilly Factor*. Media Matters reported that O'Reilly's advertising had experienced "a drastic plummet overall," suggesting that the campaign to exert economic pressure on Fox News to fire O'Reilly was working.[13]

In addition to these specific moves against conservative media targets, the mainstream media—CNN, MSNBC, and the 24/7 news cycle itself—seems to be dedicated to destroying Trump and his presidency. Mainstream media's constant breaking news alerts and "expert" commentary focus relentlessly on criticisms of Trump's every word, yet give little time to any accomplishments or positive news coming out of the White House.

The "Indivisible" Movement

Indivisible has risen as a hard-left grassroots partisan group dedicated to applying "Tea Party tactics" to resist and obstruct the Trump agenda, including targeting Trump-supporting GOP members of Congress and disrupting town hall meetings to visiting district congressional offices to ask questions about "racism, authoritarianism, and corruption."

Posted on the group's website is the Indivisible Guide, described as "A Practical Guide for Resisting the Trump Agenda."[14] The authors of the Indivisible Guide claim to be former progressive congressional staffers "who saw the Tea Party beat back President Obama's agenda." The guide teaches progressive activists techniques of disruption that can be applied to harass any member of the House or Senate who dares to support Trump.

Consider the first paragraph in the introduction to the guide as a statement of resistance and obstruction: "Donald Trump is the biggest popular-vote loser in history to ever call himself President. In spite of the fact that he has no mandate, he will attempt to use his congressional majority to reshape America in his own racist, authoritarian, and corrupt image. If progressives are going to stop this, we must stand indivisibly opposed to Trump and the Members of Congress (MoCs) who would do his bidding. Together, we have the power to resist—and we have the power to win."

The guide details how to stall the Trump agenda by disrupting congressional offices, realizing that a day a Trump-supporting member of Congress spends thinking about Indivisible is a day "that they're not ending Medicare, privatizing public schools, or preparing a Muslim registry." Indivisible activists seek to "sap the will of representatives to support reactionary change" by making Trump-supporting members of Congress ask repeatedly, "How am I going to explain this to the angry constituents who keep showing up at my events and demanding answers?"

The guide describes their "alternative, positive progressive agenda" as promoting "climate change awareness, economic justice, health care for all, racial equality, gender and sexual equality, and peace and human rights." To promote these goals, the Indivisible Guide recommends the following disruptive tactics: getting local news media to report that protestors barraged Trump-supporting "Congresswoman Sara" with questions about the infrastructure, or that angry constituents strongly objected to "Congressman Bob's" support for privatizing Medicare.

As for recruits, the Invisible Guide suggests that progressive activists target "those most directly threatened by the Trump agenda," including immigrants, people of color, LGBT people, the poor and working class, and women. "If you are forming a group, we urge you to make a conscious effort to pursue diversity and solidarity at every stage in the process," the Indivisible Guide advises. Progressive activists are encouraged to use the "indivisible" name in forming local groups, such as the "Springfield Indivisible against Hate," but progressive activists are equally free to pick their own group names, as long as the name includes the geographical area of the group, "so it's clear that you're rooted in the community."

The Indivisible Guide admonishes progressive activists to agree in advance on a simple message as the focus for disrupting a particular town hall meeting or local community photo opportunity with a Trump-supporting politician. "Coordinate with each other to chant this message during any public remarks your member of Congress makes," the guide advises. "This can be difficult and a bit uncomfortable. But it sends a powerful message to your member of Congress that they won't be able to get press for other concerns until they address your concerns."

Whether the Indivisible disruption involves a town hall meeting, a visit to the member of Congress's district office, or a barrage of coordinated phone calls designed to tie up phone lines in the district office, the Indivisible Guide reminds progressive activists that the "optics" of events are all important. Sit-ins, for instance, can backfire, the Indivisible Guide insists, admonishing that "you are working best when you are protesting an issue that affects you and/or members of your group (e.g. seniors and caregivers on Medicare cuts, or Muslims and allies protesting a Muslim registry)."

The concluding paragraphs appear aimed at an assumed generation of maturing politically correct millennials:

> We wrote this guide because we believe that the coming years will see an unprecedented movement of Americans rising up across the country to protect our values, our neighbors, and ourselves. Our goal is to provide practical understanding of how your Members of Congress (MoCs) think, and how you can demonstrate to them the depth and power of the opposition to Donald Trump and to Republican congressional overreach. This is not a panacea, and it is not intended to stand alone. We strongly urge you to marry the strategy in this guide with a broader commitment to creating a more just society, building local power, and addressing systemic injustice and racism.
>
> Finally, this guide is intended as a work in progress, one that we hope to continue updating as the resistance to the Trump agenda takes shape.

While Indivisible disavows being funded by George Soros directly, Matthew Vadum, senior vice president at the Capital Research Center, has discovered that at least three of the group's principals have worked for Soros-funded organizations.[15]

The impression Indivisible wanted to convey was that town halls and local meetings with GOP members of Congress during congressional recesses that were disrupted by attendees angry over President Trump's plan to "repeal and replace" Obamacare involved spontaneous outbursts of concern expressed by ordinary citizens. However, on February 21, 2017, Trump tweeted the obvious: "The so-called angry crowds in home districts of some Republicans are actually, in numerous cases, planned out by liberal activists. Sad!"

The truth is that these disruptive tactics were not genuine expressions of voter grassroots politics but highly organized events that included coordination with Obama activists at his Organizing for Action (OFA) organization, the successor to Organizing for America, a group that Obama created for his 2008 presidential campaign. The mainstream media presentation of disruptive town hall meetings was designed to convince the public the #NeverTrump movement was large and growing. But just like the anti-Trump hecklers and street thugs trying to disrupt or prevent Trump rallies during the presidential campaign or Antifa street thugs seeking to prevent GOP loyalists from attending Trump's Inaugural Ball, the Indivisible protest events are carefully orchestrated and staged. Protestors trying to disrupt town hall meetings run by Trump-supporting GOP members of Congress have included dedicated hard-left activists recruited from left-leaning organizations as diverse as Black Lives Matter, George Soros–funded MoveOn.org, union workers recruited from the Service Employees International Union (SEIU), and Planned Parenthood supporters.[16]

CHAPTER 10

Antifa Anarchists Go Wild

Everywhere a Battlefield.

—title of a Red Guards Austin blogpost,
August 2017

POLICE ACROSS THE UNITED States are being forced to deal with a new hard-left, communist-derived movement organized under the code word *Antifa*, which is short for "antifascist." On June 12, 2017, the New Jersey Department of Homeland Security (DHS) and Preparedness officially declared Antifa to be a terrorist group, explaining the following: "Anti-fascist groups or 'Antifa,' are a subset of the anarchist movement and focus on issues involving racism, sexism, and anti-Semitism, as well as other perceived injuries." The New Jersey DHS stressed that the Antifa movement is opposed to "fascism, racism, and law enforcement" while targeting in particular far-right extremists, including perceived white supremacists.[1]

On September 1, 2017, Politico disclosed that previously unreported documents revealed that the US DHS designated the activities of Antifa as "domestic terrorist violence," a conclusion reached in a previously undisclosed April 2016 DHS/FBI joint intelligence assessment.[2] The assessment concluded that Antifa "anarchist extremists" were the primary instigators of violence at public rallies against a wide range of targets, including police, government, and political institutions, along with symbols of the capitalist system, racism, social injustice, and fascism.[3]

Despite this designation as a domestic terrorist group, the mainstream media has continued to champion the Antifa movement as if the group were a freedom-fighting organization. The partisan mainstream media portrays Antifa as if the group were standing on moral high ground in justifiable opposition to reactionary white supremacist groups seen as espousing a combination of racist, nationalist, and populist sentiments on the extreme far-right. The violent, confrontational nature of Antifa anarchists presents a challenge to US law enforcement that is unprecedented. The hard-left violent extremists leading the Antifa movement reject the free speech principles on which American civil discourse depends. The ultimate goal of the Antifa extremists is to achieve the demise of the US Constitution by creating anarchy in the streets.

Antifa in Austin, Texas: "Everywhere a Battlefield"

The Antifa movement is a self-described Marxist-Leninist-Maoist collective that bears a strong resemblance to the Red Guards, a youthful student-based paramilitary social movement organized by Chairman Mao Zedong in communist China's Cultural Revolution of 1966–67.

In an attempt to reinvigorate China's communist revolution of 1945 49, thousands of Chinese youth clad in military fatigues roamed the streets of major cities during China's Cultural Revolution. These Red Guard activists closed universities, destroyed churches, burned libraries, tore down statues and historical monuments, and ransacked private homes in an attempt to destroy the "four olds"—old ideas, old customs, old habits, and old culture. In what became a civil war between the generations in China, somewhere between half a million and two million people lost their lives in a Cultural Revolution that Chinese radicals hoped would "lead the planet into communism."[4]

The Red Guards Austin, an Antifa group gaining prominence in the Texas Antifa movement, openly advocates for violent revolution against capitalism. The group proclaims in a blog titled "Everywhere a Battlefield" that weapons training is needed for a war that is "here and now" entering a phase of revolutionary violence.[5] Red Guard Texas mixes a fluid, slogan-driven communist ideology to identify President Trump as a white supremacist by charging that Trump embraces Nazi fascist politics. The Antifa movement has found a perfect formula to justify street thugs being dressed in black gear from head to toe, with bandanas that hide their identities. Dressed as terrorists, Antifa anarchists engage in the type of street violence that leftist revolutionaries have identified with toppling governments since the days of Lenin and the Russian Revolution of 1917.

At a fundraising event on September 7, 2016, Hillary Clinton was recorded on video making one of the most defining statements of the presidential campaign. "You know, to just be grossly generalistic, you could put half of Trump's supporters into what I call the basket of deplorables. Right?" she said to what the *New York Times* reported was a combination of applause and laughter. She continued, "The racist, sexist, homophobic, xenophobic, Islamaphobic—you name it. And unfortunately, there are people like that. And he has lifted them up."[6]

With this pronouncement, Hillary Clinton made clear that the Marxist analysis of class conflict in the United States had moved from a 1930s focus championing the working people of the labor union movement to focusing on the oppressed as defined by leftist identity politics. The new victims were no longer working-class poor but women and "people of color." The oppressor stayed the same—namely, the imperialistic, capitalistic, colonialist, war-mongering state, as epitomized by "white males" exercising their "white privilege." Antifa has embraced this Marxist shift, targeting Donald Trump as the fascist "Hater in Chief" leading a reactionary army consisting of Hillary Clinton's "basket of deplorables." Again, put simply, the Antifa revolutionaries assumed the politically correct moral high ground in their opposition to the racist, sexist, homophobic, xenophobic, and Islamaphobic voters supporting Trump.

The Antifa movement shares much with both the anti-globalization protests against the World Trade Organization in Seattle, Washington, in November 1999 and the Occupy movement that staged sit-in protests in Zuccotti Park in New York City's Wall Street financial district in September 2011. But since the election of Donald Trump as president, the Antifa movement in America has assumed the position as the radical left's paramilitary arm of the #Resistance #Obstruct movement determined to oust President Trump from the White House.

"Fascist Go Home!"

As noted earlier, on Inauguration Day, January 20, 2017, Antifa thugs, most dressed in black from head to toe and wearing masks or bandanas hiding their faces, launched violent street protests in Washington, DC, in an attempt to "shut down" Donald Trump's swearing-in ceremony and prevent the Trump faithful from attending Inaugural Balls.

In what was branded as a "DisruptJ20" protest, some 1,000 Antifa thugs broke windows at Starbucks, McDonalds, and Bank of America as well as in commercial buildings in downtown Washington. Antifa rioters flooded streets, blocked traffic, burned trash, and broke windshields of passing cars. The continuous flow of confrontational, in-your-face insults—made even more threatening because they consisted of angry, vulgar, and personally degrading language—continued into the night, with Antifa activists harassing Trump supporters trying to make their way into the DC convention center to attend the evening's main Inaugural Ball.

Washington police, armed with batons and wearing protective helmets and riot gear, responded en masse, determined to clear the streets of protestors by using tear gas and pepper spray. Still, lasting until the early morning hours, a violent rampage started two blocks from the White House and spread to McPherson Square and K Street. A stretch limousine was set on fire at K and 13th Streets after protestors threw a flare through its shattered windows. Six police officers were injured and some 230 rioters were arrested after the violent protests broke out that afternoon and continued through the evening. Rioters sought to bring traffic throughout the city to a halt and attempted to close all entrances to the DC Convention Hall. As an indication of the seriousness of the violence, protesters who were arrested were charged with felonious rioting—an offense that carries a maximum penalty 10 years in prison plus $25,000 in fines.[7]

Next, Antifa claimed success in Berkeley, California, when protestors prevented conservative activist Milo Yiannopoulos from speaking on February 2, 2017.[8] Two months later, in April 2017, Antifa groups staged a violent protest in Portland, Oregon, that caused the city to cancel the annual Rose Festival in which the Multnomah County Republican Party planned to participate—a move that granted Antifa another victory.[9] Then on August 15–17, 2017, in Charleston, South Carolina, Antifa members counterprotested at a "Unite the Right" rally seeking to preserve a Civil War statue of Confederate General Robert E. Lee.

Antifa violence returned to Berkeley in August 2017. Apparently ignorant or unconcerned with the history of the leftist "free speech movement" in Berkeley, California, in the 1960s, a group of black-clad Antifa anarchists wearing masks disrupted a free-speech event organized in Berkeley's Martin Luther King Jr. Civic Center Park by the Oregon-based Patriot Prayer—a group the mainstream media portrayed as "a right-wing organization" that "has organized other events that have attracted white supremacists and ended up in violent confrontations among demonstrators on both sides."[10]

The small group of conservative "free speech" protestors were outnumbered by a larger crowd of some 2,000 Antifa counterprotestors determined to "Rally against Hate" by denying "racist right-wing white supremacists supporting Trump" the opportunity to hold a small, peaceful event. "A pepper-spray-wielding Trump supporter was smacked to the ground with homemade shields," the *Washington Post* reported. "Another was attacked by five black-clad Antifa members, each wind-milling kicks and punches into a man desperately trying to protect himself. A conservative leader retreated for safety behind a line of riot police as marchers chucked water bottles, shot off pepper spray, and screamed, 'Fascist go home!'"[11]

Undercover videos made by James O'Keefe's Project Veritas during the DC Inaugural Day Antifa protests made clear that the Antifa protestors are not "university students," as was the case in the 1960s protests at universities against the Vietnam War, but professional agitators willing to engage in criminal activity to disrupt Trump supporters and create chaos.[12]

The Antifa movement as it has taken shape in the United States practices a type of street violence that draws from Saul Alinsky's radical "community organizing" ideas. Alinsky taught leftist "to rub raw social and racial class tensions" in order to delegitimize the US Constitution. Antifa's goal is to bring down the Trump administration by causing the type of violent political anarchy the Antifa movement believes will lead to the creation of a communist or socialist utopia right here in the United States of America.[13] The logic of the hard-left demands that Trump be seen as a Nazi on the right, a nationalist who secretly wishes to impose a white supremacist totalitarian government on the United States. This logic ignores the fact that Trump is a center-right politician. As noted earlier, Adolph Hitler in 1930s Germany rose from a national socialist party, as made clear by the formal name of the Nazi party in German, the *Nationalsozialistische Deutsche Arbeiterparti* (NSDAP), a name that stresses the Nazis were both a nationalist, German-first movement and socialists believing in a state-controlled welfare state.

Political Correctness Champions Antifa

On August 13, 2017, when at a press conference in Bridgewater, New Jersey, President Trump condemned the "egregious display of hatred, bigotry, and violence from many sides." He was immediately excoriated by the mainstream media for condemning Antifa in terms that were morally equivalent to his condemnation of neo-Nazi white supremacist groups.

Those on the radical left, for instance, have argued that Robert Spencer's "white pride" legitimates characterizing Spencer as a neo-Nazi, a KKK member, and a white supremacist—all associations Spencer denies—as well as justifying violence against him. This explains an incident where Spencer was sucker-punched in his face while he was giving an interview to a journalist on the streets of Washington, DC, during the inauguration festivities.[14]

The mainstream media has jumped on the politically correct bandwagon, proclaiming the *alt-right*—a new term the hard-left has grabbed to condemn conservatives and libertarians as white supremacist racists—is an extreme view that must be countered by extreme measures, including Antifa violence designed to prevent any person or group the hard-left tags as "alt-right" from exercising traditional First Amendment free speech rights.

In November 2016, the Associated Press issued new guidelines that require reference to groups designated "alt-right" as racist, with a requirement that whenever "alt-right" is used in a story, writers must include the definition, "an offshoot of conservativism mixing racism, white nationalism, and populism," or more simply, "a white nationalist movement."[15]

In an article published on the Associate Press blog, John Daniszewski, vice president for standards for the Associated Press, described the "alt-right" as follows:

> The "alt-right" or "alternative right" is a name currently embraced by some white supremacists and white nationalists to refer to themselves and their ideology, which emphasizes preserving and protecting the white race in the United States in addition to, or over, other traditional conservative positions such as limited government, low taxes and strict law-and-order.
>
> The movement has been described as a mix of racism, white nationalism and populism.

Although many adherents backed President-elect Donald Trump in the recent election, Trump last week said he disavows and condemns the "alt-right."

The movement criticizes "multiculturalism" and more rights for non-whites, women, Jews, Muslims, gays, immigrants and other minorities. Its members reject the American democratic ideal that all should have equality under the law regardless of creed, gender, ethnic origin or race.[16]

The Associated Press has issued no guidelines requiring that the Antifa movement be designated as a terrorist organization on the extreme political left that espouses the use of violence. Instead, Daniszewski has issued much more sympathetic guidelines for writers wanting to report on the Antifa movement: "Finally, a term has emerged in the news recently—an umbrella description for the far-left-leaning militant groups that resist neo-Nazis and white supremacists at demonstrations and other events. The movement calls itself Antifa, a contraction for anti-fascists, and emulates historic anti-fascist actors in Europe going back to the 1930s."[17]

"Prolonged silence about the left's violence is dangerous," former House speaker Newt Gingrich wrote in a Fox News editorial published August 31, 2017. "It is time for the national media to reflect and start condemning leftwing attacks just as vehemently as it does the brutality of Neo-Nazis, the KKK, and other hateful groups." Gingrich's point was simple, but important, if the United States is to have any chance of preserving First Amendment free speech rights amid the violent resistance the political left has decided to exercise to obstruct the Trump administration from governing. "Violence in all forms is wrong and must be harshly rebuked by all Americans," Gingrich concluded.[18]

PART 3

How Trump Wins

CHAPTER 11

How Trump Can Win the Propaganda War

Those who are capable of tyranny are capable of perjury to sustain it.

—Lysander Spooner

THE CENTRAL PREMISE OF this book is that President Trump is the target of a coup d'état being undertaken by the Deep State, including the CIA, NSA, and other intelligence agencies that maintain a commitment to a globalist New World Order.

That Deep State operates secretly in cooperation with the Federal Reserve, the Comptroller of the Currency, as well as federal law enforcement agencies including the FBI and the DOJ to allow the Deep State to pursue clandestine operations, including illicit drug dealing and supplying weapons to terrorist groups, that further the "New World Order" goals of the international globalist elite. This global elite currently controls a number of important international organizations, including the United Nations, the International Monetary Fund, and the European Union. The Deep State maintains its secrecy through the willing cooperation of a corporate-owned and government-controlled mainstream.

The devastating loss of Hillary Clinton in the presidential election of 2016 set the Deep State into a panic. As a result, its agents formed and began to implement a plan they hoped would remove Donald Trump from the presidency.

Deep State Propaganda

To achieve this goal, the Deep State and the mainstream media are employing classic techniques of propaganda and disinformation that were first utilized by Nazi Germany in the 1930s and advanced and perfected by the Soviet Union during the Cold War. The first principle of all propaganda and disinformation involves the manipulation of public opinion by the creation of a lie—known in today's terminology as a *narrative* or a *meme*—that is crafted to be sufficiently credible so that a persistent campaign of repeating the lie can change public opinion, even if the narrative is totally untrue, concocted without any basis in fact, evidence, or reality.

As noted earlier, in 1928, Edward L. Bernays, widely considered the father of public relations, wrote a book titled *Propaganda: The Making of the Public Mind* that greatly influenced the thinking of Joseph Goebbels, the minister of propaganda for Nazi Germany from 1933 to 1945.[1] When approached by Goebbels to advise Nazi Germany, Bernays refused, concerned about how his book would be used. But Bernays's refusal did not deter the Nazis. Using Bernays's book for evil, Goebbels crafted a meme drawing from the "science" of eugenics emerging in the 1930s to vilify Jews, resulting in the horror of the Holocaust, in which an estimated six million Jews were brutally murdered.

In 1966, the Soviet Union backed philosopher Bertrand Russell in holding an international tribunal on Vietnam War crimes that advanced the argument ultimately picked up by John Kerry and the group Vietnam Veterans Against the War. In January and February 1971, Kerry held a "Winter Soldiers Investigation" based on the Bertrand Russell model. This culminated in Kerry's testimony to the Fulbright Committee on April 22, 1971, in which he defamed the US military fighting in Vietnam by telling the Senate Foreign Relations Committee that American soldiers in Vietnam had "raped, cut off ears, cut off heads, taped wires from portable telephones to human genitals and turned up the power, cut off limbs, blown up bodies, randomly shot at civilians, razed villages in a fashion reminiscent of Genghis Kahn."

Ion Mihai Pacepa, a former three-star general in the secret police of communist Romania—one of the highest-ranking Soviet-bloc intelligence agents to defect to the United States—recognized Kerry's claims as deriving from a Russian KGB disinformation campaign. In his 2013 book *Disinformation*, Pacepa argued that KGB *dezinformatsiya* launched the political career of Senator

John Kerry, the 2004 Democratic Party presidential candidate. "Although Senator Kerry never fully revealed the source of those outrageous accusations (that Kerry made to the Fulbright Committee), I recognized them as being the product of another KGB disinformation operation," Pacepa wrote. "In the 1960s and '70s, when I was a leader of the Soviet bloc intelligence community, the KGB spread those same vitriolic accusations, almost word for word, throughout American and European leftist movements. They were part of a KGB disinformation operation aimed at discouraging the United States from protecting the world against communist expansion."[2]

"Russian Collusion": A Deep State Propaganda Narrative

The current disinformation meme being advanced by the Deep State and mainstream media is the "Russian collusion," which maintains that Donald Trump colluded with the Russians to hack emails from the Democratic National Party as a tactic employed to defeat Hillary Clinton. The argument initially advanced by Hillary Clinton during the 2016 presidential campaign was that the "collusion" involved Donald Trump somehow working with the Russians to hack internal emails from the DNC and from John Podesta that contained damaging admissions.

As the meme advanced, the Democrats and the mainstream media began accepting almost any connection that could be established between the Trump campaign and a Russian as "proof" that Trump had colluded with the Russians, including just the suggestion that Trump might want to meet with someone who could connect the campaign to Russian opposition research that might damage the Clinton campaign.

In the world of disinformation, it does not matter that Senator Diane Feinstein (Democrat, California) said publicly on May 4 that the Senate Select Committee on Intelligence had seen no evidence of collusion between Donald Trump's campaign aides and Russian officials[3] or that the former director of national intelligence James Clapper told a Senate judiciary subcommittee on May 8 that he still had not seen any evidence of any kind of collusion between the Trump campaign and Russian foreign nationals.[4] As has been stressed repeatedly throughout this book, no public official in the US intelligence apparatus or Congress has produced any credible evidence that the Trump campaign ever colluded with Russia in a meaningful way that could possibly have caused Hillary Clinton to lose the presidential election. The argument remains that Hillary was a terrible candidate, campaigning on themes of leftist identity politics that did not resonate sufficiently with the electorate.

When Special Counselor Mueller indicted former Trump campaign chair Paul Manafort and former Trump campaign official Rick Gates on October 27, 2017, the charges involved failing to register as foreign agents under the Foreign Agents Registration Unit, a charge that had nothing to do with the Russian collusion propaganda meme. Mueller further charged Manafort with laundering money into the United States through offshore banks from work Manafort and Gates did for Ukraine in a contract that ended in 2014, two years before Trump officially declared his candidacy for president. Again, these allegations might be relevant to tax evasion charges, but they had nothing to do with Hillary losing the election.

Harvard law professor Alan Dershowitz has repeatedly explained that even if it could be proved, there is "no law on the books" that would make colluding with the Russians a crime.[5] This is the first sign we are dealing with disinformation—namely, there is no evidence for the claim. In fact, the claim cannot even be specified other than to suggest that somehow, Trump stole emails from the DNC and John Podesta that, once purloined, were delivered to Julian Assange at WikiLeaks for public dissemination. However, Assange has repeatedly denied that Donald Trump or Russia were his sources. Again, the damage caused by the WikiLeaks publications came not from the fact that the emails were stolen but from the detrimental exchanges Podesta and other campaign officials had in emails they foolishly imagined would forever remain secret.

Even when evidence proving the meme false is produced, the skilled Deep State propagandist can keep the meme going by qualifying the claim, ever so slightly, as to leave open the possibility that it could yet be proven true, if only the public could get access to the "real information."

Representative Adam Schiff (Democrat, California), the ranking member of the House Permanent Select Committee on Intelligence, first began countering the "no evidence" fact with an assertion that there is "circumstantial evidence" of collusion between the Trump campaign and Russia—a statement he made on NBC's *Meet the Press* for the first time on March 17, 2017.[6] In his next move, Schiff pressured the House Intelligence Committee chairman Devin Nunes (Republican, California) to temporarily remove himself from the "Russian collusion" investigation after the House Ethics Committee decided to investigate whether Nunes may have made unauthorized disclosures of classified information following his controversial visit to the White House to review reports suggesting that the Obama administration had Trump campaign officials under electronic surveillance.[7]

The Deep State knows the "Russian collusion" accusations against Trump lacks proof, but still the mainstream media simply refuses to print evidence that it was Hillary Clinton and John Podesta who were being paid by Russia or that Democratic National Committee computer expert Seth Rich was the one who most likely stole the DNC emails from the inside, leaking copies to Julian Assange at WikiLeaks. This leads us to formulate two propaganda rules.

Propaganda Rule #1: **Any facts that disprove the disinformation meme false are rejected as not definitive because the investigation is continuing and proof might yet be found.**

As a corollary, those who doubt the propaganda meme are chastised as conspiracy theorists—a label designed to disparage anyone bold enough to have perceived the truth. It is essential to understand that a well-crafted disinformation meme like the "Russian collusion" narrative is impossible to dislodge by facts that prove the narrative baseless, completely "without evidence," or untrue.

Propaganda Rule #2: **Anyone attempting to disprove the truth of the disinformation meme is targeted for ridicule as part of the conspiracy theory.**

As a corollary, a propaganda meme advanced in politics will be more successful if it is launched by the Democratic Party because the Democrats control the partisan mainstream media and can expect the media to advance their narrative aggressively.

All this leads to the conclusion that those attempting to defend President Trump will not advance the cause by refuting Democratic Party and mainstream media claims that the Trump campaign colluded with Russia, even though Special Counselor Mueller cannot produce an indictment and the intelligence community remains incapable of producing any evidence that Donald Trump or anyone involved with his campaign colluded with Russia.

So How Does Trump Win the Propaganda War?

In designing a counterpropaganda strategy, it is important to realize that the president of the United States is endowed by the Constitution with formidable powers. This leads us to the following two counterpropaganda rues.

Counterpropaganda Rule #1: **A propaganda campaign can only be defeated by the passage of time, as the public will lose interest in the disinformation narrative if no criminal**

convictions can be achieved by a special prosecutor's efforts after the expenditure of enormous government resources in the attempt to do so.

If Special Counselor Mueller fails to produce an indictment specifically charging someone in the Trump campaign with "Russian collusion," he will begin to justify Trump's charge that his investigation is a "witch hunt." With his first indictment against Manafort and Gates, Mueller could produce only money-laundering charges, plus a technical violation that Manafort and Gates had not properly registered with the federal government as agents of a foreign government. That Mueller's indictment against Manafort and Gates did not even include charges of tax evasion strongly suggests Mueller is already losing the propaganda battle.

In his second indictment, announced the same day as the Manafort/Gates indictment, Mueller indicted a minor player in the Trump campaign, George Papadopoulos, not for colluding with Russia but for lying to the FBI. When it turned out that the Trump campaign did not act on Papadopoulos's recommendation to meet with Russian officials to get opposition research on Hillary Clinton, the effort to make the Papadopoulos indictment a bombshell against Trump fell flat. If Mueller continues to investigate and indict Trump campaign officials for activities that preceded the 2016 presidential election, as he did in the Manafort/Gates indictment, pressure will build on Congress to call on the Justice Department to terminate Mueller's authority as special counselor.

Counterpropaganda Rule #2: **Realizing that the presidency is endowed with enormous powers, a president must take action to change the subject by action aimed at addressing a legitimate national security crisis.**

It is a proven fact of US history since the end of World War II that presidential action in a legitimate national security

emergency will take all the air out of a well-crafted disinformation meme, forcing Deep State actors and the mainstream media
to devote their attention to the crisis the president has decided to
address. The one caution here is that the national emergency must
be legitimate and serious. Simply launching a few cruise missiles
at a supposed terrorist camp in the middle of a Middle Eastern
desert runs the risk of being classified as a "wag-the-dog" diver-
sion. This was proven by President Clinton's failure to change the
subject by bombing terrorists in Afghanistan and Sudan in 1998,
three days after he was forced to admit to having an inappropriate sexual relationship with Monica Lewinsky.[8]

The point of this rule is to take control of the news cycle, forcing the Deep State and mainstream media coconspirators to
abandon their "Russian collusion" meme to cover a foreign policy agenda that comports with President Trump's public policy
objective of keeping America safe from foreign threats.

FORTIFY TRUMP'S LEGAL DEFENSE

In the background, the Trump administration must lawyer up,
seeking the advice of top private law firms. Trump must make
sure charges brought forward by Democrats in Congress to
advance impeachment efforts are countered in Congressional
hearings by lawyers skillful enough to expose to the American
public how and why Hillary Clinton and her supporters advanced
the "Russian collusion" meme without evidence simply to excuse
her inadequacies as a presidential candidate.

Countering the Deep State and the mainstream media by
fighting a street-by-street battle in Congressional hearings is a
type of hand-to-hand combat that delays the advancement of the
"Russian collusion" meme. This tactic has a better chance of successfully combatting the Deep State's propaganda attack than
trying to make the meme go away by arguing alternative facts as
an overall theory of political reality.

USE THE POWERS OF THE PRESIDENCY TO THE FULLEST

Counterpropaganda Rules #1 and #2 involve designing a plan of action that takes control of the news cycle, forcing the Deep State and mainstream media coconspirators to abandon their "Russian collusion" meme to cover news that President Trump wants covered. A foreign policy agenda that comports with President Trump's public policy objective of keeping America safe from foreign threats need not be confined to North Korea and Iran. Should the Trump administration begin serious peace discussions in the Middle East between Israel and Palestine, a new power structure might be created in the Middle East. Conceivably, President Trump could leverage the willingness of the United States to abandon military action in Afghanistan in exchange for Russia agreeing to contain Iran.

In 1986, when President Reagan met with Mikhail Gorbachev, leader of the Soviet Union, in Reykjavík, Iceland, a project known as "Star Wars"—America's Strategic Defensive Initiative (SDI)— dominated the news cycle, with the mainstream media forced to cover the summit and Reagan's subsequent failure to come to an agreement with Gorbachev. Only the president is capable of bold foreign policy action, and President Trump needs to learn how to play this card to his advantage—silencing memes backed by no evidence that are aimed at destroying his presidency.

On the domestic side, President Trump can continue stimulating the economy by relaxing and/or eliminating Obama administrative regulatory decisions. On March 13, 2017, Trump signed an executive order mandating a "Comprehensive Plan for Reorganizing the Executive Branch." On his own authority as chief executive, President Trump could require various cabinet members to announce plans for making dramatic reductions in force (RIFs), downsizing agencies unpopular to Trump's base, like the EPA or the Department of Education, to shadows of their former selves.

Understanding the power of the bureaucracy to achieve Deep State goals by setting rules and regulations that required neither

Congressional legislation nor Supreme Court approval, President Obama aimed to set a record for the size of the federal workforce, leaving office with more than 1.7 million people collecting government salaries in civilian agencies in 2017.[9] As a measure of the Obama administration's enthusiasm for achieving Deep State objectives through bureaucratic action, consider that the printed version of the "Federal Register," the government's record of all rules and regulations currently in effect, topped off at an all-time record of 97,110 pages on the last federal workday of 2016, dwarfing the previous record of 81,405 pages that Obama set in 2010 by 15,705 pages.[10]

President Trump must understand that bureaucrats are natural allies of the Deep State. Seeking to maintain their jobs for decades, bureaucrats devote their time and energy to legislating outside the authority granted to the executive branch by the Constitution. Writing and publishing countless rules and regulations, bureaucrats silently implement Deep State dictates to expand the size of the bureaucracy so as to extend federal government control into every corner of life in the United States. The only way to eliminate Deep State control over the federal bureaucracy is to massively reduce its size, firing thousands of bureaucrats through RIFs that bypass civil service regulations designed to protect bureaucrats from job termination. Whole departments can be closed or consolidated.

The point is that President Trump must realize legacy employees in the bureaucracy remain loyal to the Clintons and to the Obamas. Given their ideological certainty, these bureaucrats are the foot soldiers in the hard-left's war to resist and obstruct the Trump agenda.

STIMULATE THE ECONOMY

Pushing a historic tax cut through Congress would also dominate the news cycle with reports that the American public would most likely receive enthusiastically. One tax cut this year can be followed by another massive tax cut next year. Through a combination of eliminating federal regulations and the federal bureaucracy, plus getting Congress to pass a series of tax cuts, Trump can make sure the American economy thrives.

To the extent that the economy remains strong, President Trump will retain the Middle America populist "America First" support that got him elected. The president should seriously entertain proposals to eliminate the Federal Reserve and end the federal income tax. Both are widely (and correctly) viewed as outside the scope and authority of the US Constitution. By forcing a national debate on moving to a federal tax on consumption, Trump would both dominate the news cycle in his favor and continue to stimulate the economy.

ISSUE EXECUTIVE ORDERS

Even if signing and/or implementing Trump's various executive orders risks new controversies, President Trump will force the Deep State and mainstream media to shift their focus from the "Russian collusion" meme to attack each new step the administration takes to act by executive order.

Trump has begun by issuing executive orders that roll back "legislation from the White House" that Obama put in place through extensive use of his pen. By continuing to appeal to his base of antiglobalist supporters, Trump will increase his chances of withstanding the impeachment storm the hard-left Democrats and mainstream media intend to send his way. If the American people see the executive orders as increasing domestic security, reducing crime, creating new jobs, reducing government expense, or achieving any one of a host of other important domestic policy goals, the executive orders will be popular with Trump voters, even if the establishment elites on both coasts support the Deep State / mainstream media agenda.

So Trump's decision to pull out of the Paris Climate Accord appealed to his conservative and libertarian base, who are convinced the left's "global warming / climate change" rhetoric is nothing more than a globalist ideological agenda backed by "junk science" and calculated to redistribute income worldwide by introducing a new United Nations carbon tax. A decision to stay in the Paris Climate Accord would have depressed Trump's base, encouraging the Deep State and mainstream media to believe that Trump was more vulnerable to impeachment than ever.

IGNORE MAINSTREAM MEDIA POLLS

Finally, to save his presidency, Trump should ignore mainstream media polls designed only to convince Trump voters that he is failing. These same polls dramatically underestimated Trump's popularity during the 2016 presidential campaign.

This has continued with Trump in the White House. The goal of the mainstream media in conducting and publishing polls must be regarded as partisan, with biased sampling methodologies intentionally implemented to depress Trump's favorable numbers. The truth is, the #NeverTrump resistance and obstruction campaign has failed, with Trump's base now stronger than ever. Trump supporters now see him as the victim of an insane hard-left Democratic Party that cannot accept that Hillary lost because she was a terrible candidate running on politically correct themes central to the socialist identity politics that Trump voters rejected.

If the election were to be held a second time as 2016 wound down, Trump would most likely win again—only this time, by an even larger margin of victory.

CHAPTER 12

The Counteroffensive Trump Must Launch

Also, there is NO COLLUSION!

—Donald J. Trump, October 2017

THE MAINSTREAM MEDIA DEPENDS on daily attacks that advance the "Russian collusion" meme with disclosures that are sufficiently alarming to dominate the news cycle for at least 24 hours. It does not matter to the mainstream media that these daily attacks on Trump are not true or, if true, petty—of the type the mainstream media would never have made against Barack Obama or Hillary Clinton. All that matters is that the new disclosures advance the "Russian collusion" meme that the Deep State is betting will culminate in Trump being impeached.

Lawfare

Julian Assange of WikiLeaks fame has defined the term *lawfare* to mean the abuse of the law to obtain ends traditionally met through war, such as, in the case of the #NeverTrump resistance and obstruction movement, seizing control of the government. The word *lawfare* accurately describes the coup d'état the Deep State is attempting to pull off, with the hard-left of the Democratic Party and the mainstream media working together to Trump from office through indictments brought by Special Prosecutor Robert Mueller.

The ultimate goal of Mueller's "witch hunt" remains to charge Trump with obstructing justice for firing FBI Director James Comey. The plot involves forcing Trump to defend himself against the criminal charges Mueller plans to bring against him in federal court or to force a constitutional crisis if Trump demands that instead of a federal prosecution in a US district court, impeachment proceedings must be brought in the House so he could be tried in the Senate.[1]

As discussed in the previous chapter, Ion Mihai Pacepa, the former three-star general in the secret police of communist Romania, one of the highest-ranking Soviet-bloc intelligence agents to defect to the United States, was a master in the art of propaganda disinformation. In his 2013 book *Disinformation*, Pacepa discussed the last meeting he had with former general secretary of the Communist Party of the Soviet Union Yuri Andropov in the 1970s, when Andropov was a KGB chairman. As Pacepa relates the meeting, Andropov told him, "Now all we have to do is keep this machinery alive," referring to the disinformation campaign that prompted the European Marxists to take to the streets to protest America's war on terrorism. Pacepa comments that Andropov was "a shrewd judge of human nature" who knew when a plan was about to succeed. "He understood that in the end the Soviet's original involvement [in the propaganda campaign designed to descript the United States in Europe] would be forgotten, and then the *dezinformatsiya* machinery would take on a life of its own," Pacepa wrote. "That was just the way human nature worked."[1]

There is only one way to defeat a propaganda attack, and that is to counterattack. The counterattack must focus on the agents responsible for launching the propaganda disinformation attack in the first place.

Turn the Tables on the Democrats

To defeat the false "Russia collusion" narrative, Trump must begin criminal prosecutions against Hillary Clinton and her supporters, including the Podesta brothers, John and Tony. Ultimately Trump must seek the appointment of a special prosecutor to go after the lying hard-left Democrats conspiring to impeach him, but the criminal investigation Trump launches must include scandals such as the Uranium One affair and plots including those launched by the Democrats to profit by selling US military technology to Russia under the guise of Secretary Clinton's "Russian reset" policy.

The Clinton Foundation must face a serious international criminal investigation to avoid the permanent damage the Clintons have done worldwide to honest, charitable giving. A criminal investigation must identify and indict those in the IRS responsible for targeting conservative and libertarian organizations and allowing George Soros and myriad other leftist foundations to enjoy tax-exempt advantages while funding a radical socialist political agenda.

The investigation must out Deep State actors, including the NSA's massive illegal surveillance of the US domestic population and the Obama administration's illegal unmasking of information gathered on political opponents from intelligence agency electronic surveillance. Trump's counterattack must expose the political corruption now at the heart of agencies including the FBI, the Department of Justice, and the Environmental Protection Agency, which the Obama administration weaponized to go after conservative and libertarian enemies. The effort must extend to expose the FBI for systematic leaks to the press undertaken to allow the Department of Justice to prosecute political opponents in the press. Social media giants, including Facebook, Twitter, and Google/YouTube must be investigated for employing algorithms that screen out or otherwise suppress conservative and libertarian postings.

Between the Uranium One scandal and the sale of military technology to Russia that Hillary and Podesta orchestrated with Skolkovo under the "reset" policy, there is plenty to investigate. For evidence, a special prosecutor could begin examining the various cash payments delivered to Hillary Clinton through the Clinton Foundation and to Podesta via the Joule shell corporations in the Netherlands. The Democrats may end up ironically being the victims of their own propaganda campaign. But Trump will need to appoint a special prosecutor given that the DOJ, already thoroughly penetrated by Deep State operatives, has repeatedly given the Clintons a pass on every investigation ever opened on them.

The Deep State roots run deep, with the CIA involved in profiting from the international drug trade, while the CIA and the Department of Treasury turn a blind eye to monitoring the massive money laundering being excused by bureaucrats who allow international bank transfers to operate illegally with impunity. The Deep State has managed to control both parties, with President Trump finding that the GOP elite leadership in Washington and New York is as committed to globalist open borders as are the hard-left political activists that have seized control of the Democratic Party.

Rooting the Deep State corruption out of the US government will not be easy, but the future of the Constitutional Republic we know as the United States of America depends on Donald J. Trump having the courage, determination, and grace of God to counterattack expeditiously and with a conviction to fight to the end these entrenched enemies of God, freedom, and humanity.

The Money-Laundering Case That Haunts the Mueller Indictments

As covered more thoroughly earlier in this book, the 2012 Department of Justice settlement with the international bank HSBC over hundreds of millions of dollars in criminal money laundering for drug cartels and terrorist groups identified with Iran hang like a sword of Damocles over Special Prosecutor Robert Mueller's indictment of Paul Manafort and Rick Gates. The settlement, announced in a Department of Justice press release dated December 11, 2012, involved a deferred prosecution agreement in which HSBC admitted criminal responsibility for laundering at least $881 million through the US financial system as well as an unspecified amount of money from federally sanctioned countries including Iran, Cuba, Sudan, Libya, and Burma.[3] In exchange for the Department of Justice agreeing not to file criminal indictments against HSBC's directors, officers, or employees, HSBC agreed to pay $1.256 billion as part of the deferred prosecution agreement, plus another $665 million in civil penalties, while admitting criminal violations of the Bank Secrecy Act (BSA), the International Emergency Economic Powers Act (IEEPA), and the Trading with the Enemy Act (TWEA).

Recall that the director of the FBI at that time was Robert Mueller. Robert Comey, who later replaced Mueller in that post, was a member of the HSBC board of directors. The case was settled by Loretta Lynch, who then was the US attorney for the Eastern District of New York. The attorney general was Eric Holder. Just to make sure the case is clear, please understand that the Obama Department of Justice allowed HSBC to pay fines to avoid facing federal criminal indictments after the bank admitted criminal responsibility for helping Mexican drug cartels and terrorist organizations with ties to countries like Iran launder hundreds of millions of dollars into the US banking system from foreign sources.

Contrast this to Mueller's decision to indict Manafort and Gates on criminal money laundering charges. To begin with, Manafort and Gates have maintained that the money regarding Mueller's indictment involved payment from Ukraine for consulting services rendered that involved no illegal activity. This point is critical: unless the government can prove the money was illegally obtained, money-laundering criminal statutes do not apply. Consider the following:

- First, is not a crime for a US citizen to be paid for consulting services rendered for a foreign government.

- Second, it is not a crime for US citizens to move money earned overseas into the United States through offshore banks, even if the banks are domiciled in known offshore money-laundering jurisdictions, such as the Cayman Islands or the Seychelles.

· Third, as long as Manafort and Gates reported the income and paid all required federal taxes, it is not a crime to deposit in a US bank funds owned overseas that were moved into the US banking system via transfers involving offshore banks.

Compare this to the HSBC case, in which Mueller, Comey, Lynch, and Holder all knew the bank was involved in the criminal money laundering hundreds of millions of dollars (a vastly larger sum than was involved in the Manafort-Gates case) for heinous international narcotics cartels and terror groups resolved to kill Americans. Yet Mueller, Comey, Lynch, and Holder were satisfied to be paid a fine that to HSBC amounted to nothing more than the cost of doing business.

Why?

As ZeroHedge.com pointed out in 2015 after the revelations from a trove of secret documents from HSBC's Swiss private bank (#SwisLeaks), HSBC could no longer claim the money laundering was due to a few rogue employees and a loosely enforced anti-money laundering policy. "The truth is that a considerable portion of the global banking system is explicitly dedicated to handling the enormous volume of cash produced daily by dope traffickers," ZeroHedge.com noted. The Senate Permanent Subcommittee on Investigations concluded that HSBC also had a long-standing relationship with Saudi Arabia's al-Rajhi bank, described by the CIA in 2003 as a "conduit for extremist finance."[4] US intelligence had assessed that al-Rajhi founder Sulaiman bin Abdul Aziz al-Rajhi was "a member of Osama bin Laden's 'Golden Chain' financiers of al-Qaeda, and had in that capacity pushed al-Rajhi bank to find ways to avoid subjecting the bank's charitable donations to official scrutiny."[5]

Finally, since the Vietnam War, HSBC was the CIA's money-laundering bank of choice to launder the proceeds the CIA was deriving from running the international heroin trade originating in Southeast Asia. Journalist and political activist Dean Henderson documented the following in his 2007 book *Big Oil and Their Bankers in the Persian Gulf: Four Horsemen, Eight Families, and Their Global Intelligence, Narcotics, and Terror Network*: "Formerly known as Hong Kong Shanghai Bank Corporation, HSBC has served as the world's #1 drug money laundry since its inception as a repository for British Crown opium proceeds accrued during the Chinese Opium Wars. During the Vietnam War, HSBC laundered CIA heroin proceeds."[6]

Peter Dale Scott, in his 2014 book *The American Deep State: Big Money, Big Oil, and the Struggle for U.S. Democracy*, made a similar observation: "Since World War II the CIA has made systemic us of drug trafficking forces to increase its covert influence—first in Thailand and Burma, then in Laos and Vietnam, and most recently in Afghanistan. With America's expansion overseas, we have seen more and more covert programs and agencies, all using drug traffickers to different and opposing ends."[7]

Evidently, with the HSBC criminal money-laundering case in 2012, FBI Director Mueller agreed with future FBI director Comey, along with then US attorneys Loretta Lynch and General Eric Holder, that it was better to let HSBC off the hook than take the risk that a fearless defense attorney would expose the CIA's role in the international drug trade. Investigative journalist Nafeez Ahmed, in a 2015 article titled "Death, Drugs and HSBC," said that it is fairly simple once one understands that "fraudulent blood money makes the world go around."[8] Matt Taibbi, writing in the *Rolling Stone* in 2013, capsulized the HSBC case in the title of his article: "Gangster Bankers: Too Big to Jail," subtitled, "How HSBC Hooked Up with Drug Traffickers and Terrorists. And Got Away with It."[9]

The HSBC settlement will haunt Mueller and his "witch hunt" once the American public realizes the Manafort-Gates prosecution is, at best, a case of technical violations in failing to register or possibly tax evasion. But the case has nothing whatsoever to do with money laundering, since consulting with Ukraine is not a crime in the United States. Rather, the goal of Mueller's indictment is to establish the pretense for undermining Donald Trump's presidency politically and possibly lead to impeachment. What we must realize from the start that even if there were evidence that the Trump campaign had colluded with Russia, there is no federal law that makes "collusion" a crime. What the HSBC criminal case and the Manafort-Gates indictment prove is that Deep State actors, including Mueller, Gates, Lynch, and Holder, can be counted on to protect their own.

Prosecution by Newspaper

Former US attorney for the Southern District of New York Preet Bharara, a Trump critic ever since the president fired him from his position, may turn out to be an unanticipated liability for Special Counselor Robert Mueller. Once Mueller added Assistant US Attorney Andrew Goldstein, one of Bharara's former top prosecutors, to his special prosecutor staff, Mueller took on the burden of explaining why he thereby implicitly condoned a pattern of illegal leaking of secret grand jury information, which has plagued Bharara's high-visibility prosecution since 2014. Specifically, Mueller may have to explain how his pattern of leaking to the press differs from the illegal leaking of grand jury information to the *New York Times* and *Washington Post* that Bharara had to admit happened in his prosecution of William T. Walters, a prominent businessman, investor, sports gambler, and philanthropist that Bharara convicted of insider trading in a US district court criminal trial that ended last July.

The federal criminal case for insider trading against noted Las Vegas–based sports gambler William T. "Billy" Walters was seriously impaired in December 2016, when the US district court judge P. Kevin Castel, in preparing to take the case to trial, learned that FBI Agent Chaves had leaked information on the case to the *New York Times* and the *Wall Street Journal* two years before Walters was indicted. What the record reveals is that despite being unable to develop enough evidence to justify a grand jury indictment regarding Walters's trading of either Clorox or Dean Foods stock, Chaves decided in April 2014 that he would prevent the investigation from going dormant by going to the press and illegally spilling juicy details from the grand jury investigation that he hoped might somehow revive the case.

When Judge Castel understood the extent of Chaves's leak, he demanded that US Attorney Bharara prepare for the court a complete accounting of the FBI leaking activity in the case—a report that Judge Castel required the US attorney's office to make public in an unsealed and nonredacted form, including the names of the reporters at the *New York Times* and the *Wall Street Journal* who cooperated with Chaves as well as a full timeline accounting for the numerous leaks both newspapers published. Thus court documents prove that US Attorney Bharara allowed the *New York Times* and *Wall Street Journal* to publish "fake news" as he prepared an insider trading case against Billy Walters.

In July, President Trump issued a volley of angry tweets after the *Washington Post* reported—again based on anonymous sources—that Trump had asked his attorneys and advisors about his ability to pardon aides, family, members, and possibly even himself as a means of "limiting or undercutting" Mueller's Russia investigation.[10] In response to the *Washington Post* story, Trump tweeted, "While we all agree the U.S. President has the complete power to pardon, why think of that when the only crime so far is LEAKS against us. FAKE NEWS."

"All Crooked Cops"

Attorney Sidney Powell, a former assistant US attorney and appellate section chief, in her 2014 book *Licensed to Lie: Exposing Corruption in the Department of Justice*, argues that prosecutorial impropriety runs rampant today among Department of Justice prosecutors, including Bharara, as well as among the lawyers recruited to Special Counselor Mueller's team. "Why did Preet Bharara prosecute Billy Walters?" Powell asked rhetorically. "Bharara prosecuted Billy Walters because Walters was a famous and hugely successful sports gambler. Because he was a multi-million-dollar investor who owned a $17 million-dollar private jet. Because Preet Bharara had suffered a series of appeals court set-backs and he valued bagging Billy Walters so he could have a new trophy to put on his wall."[11]

She noted that the trial judge in Billy Walters's case, US District Judge Castel, forced Bharara to admit that FBI Special Agent Chaves had engaged in a systematic pattern of illegally leaking grand jury information against Walters to the *New York Times* and *Wall Street Journal*, starting two years before Bharara indicted Walters. "Again, doesn't surprise me at all that prosecutors and agents in such a high-profile case leaked information," Powell responded. "Federal prosecutors often try to convict in the press before the indictment or trial." "Many top federal law enforcement officials including James Comey—and it appears Robert Mueller as well—are willing to engage in illegal acts to win convictions," she stressed. "They convince themselves or believe that someone is guilty of something, and then the end of obtaining any kind of conviction justifies whatever needs to be done to get that conviction." She continued, "Bharara, Comey, and Mueller—all three are far too political and have great powers of rationalization. Some have called them 'Dirty Cops.'"[12]

Assange Charges CIA Is Targeting
US Citizens on the Internet

On March 8, 2017, in a live-steaming internet press conference, Julian Assange announced that there are some 22,000 IP (internet protocol) addresses in the WikiLeaks database that are based in the United States, triggering Assange to suspect that the CIA has continued to go rogue, violating its charter not to investigate US citizens. "Unfortunately, the CIA does have a history of attacking not only the political parties operating overseas; the CIA has a history of acting badly within the United States as well," Assange said. "There are more than 22,000 IP addresses [in the 'Vault 7' documents] that correspond to internet systems within the United States." He continued, "We have a large project under way to determine how many of those IP addresses in the United States were attack victims and how many were intermediaries—say, an internet service provider in the United States that was attacked in order to attack someone else overseas—how may are direct victims, and how many correspond to a visitor from a foreign country to the United States, or how many correspond to a joint intelligence operation with the CIA providing technical support to an intelligence operation overseas."

A Strategy to Gain Control of the
Out-of-Control White House Press Room

Holding daily press conferences with the mainstream media sitting in the first rows of a crowded press room gives the Deep State and media agents an underserved level of respect. If the pro-Clinton, pro-Obama jackals of the mainstream media are shut out from attacking the White House press secretary on a daily basis, the mainstream loses an important stage on which to be viewed live, in real time, on cable news. Mainstream media White House correspondents should be treated as enemies, not honored celebrities, if they are resolved to act as enemies. In other words, answering questions such as "When did you stop beating your wife?" shouted out by reporters presuming the righteousness of their attacks only serves to advance the coup's narrative.

Ending daily press conferences is an important point to silencing the mainstream media by making White House press correspondents the outsiders they truly are. Currently, the White House Press room occupies the corridor attaching the White House to the West Wing, where President John Kennedy housed the White House pool in which he infamously liked to cavort naked with his favorite female assistants nicknamed "Fiddle" and "Faddle." The space is small, cramped with reporters jammed into wooden center seats too small for comfort, with broadcast equipment occupying the space at the back, and no room for all but a few representatives of privileged news outlets. The White House press secretary could easily justify announcing that the White House press room in the West Wing is being closed for renovations.

The White House press secretary should also make clear that coincident with the closing of the West Wing press room, the White House is undertaking a policy review to revise procedures for White House correspondents to obtain credentials and participate in daily press briefings. When the new policy is announced, the current West Wing press office should be closed, with a new press office opened in the Executive Office buildings across the street from the White House. Further, with daily press briefings suspended, the White House press office could resort to supplying White House correspondents with printed announcements only. These printed releases should begin by detailing requests being made by the White House legal counsel for Congress and the FBI to investigate the following:

· the extent to which the Obama administration had the Trump campaign under FISA-authorized electronic surveillance,

- the extent to which the Obama White House had "unmasked" the identity of Trump campaign officials under electronic surveillance, and

- the extent to which reports with Trump campaign officials "unmasked" were distributed within the Obama administration as well as to the press.

Over a period of a few weeks, the White House press office could lay out for the American public these serious questions regarding Hillary Clinton, her 2016 campaign, the Clinton Foundation, and John and Tony Podesta—questions designed to expose the full range of the Deep State coup d'état in progress, with the Democratic Party and the mainstream media identified as named coconspirators.

The new White House press office opened in the Executive Office buildings should be auditorium style, designed to accommodate several hundred press representatives. White House television correspondents seeking to broadcast from the White House lawn need to be moved across the street to a designated area outside the grounds. The ability of internet-based news agencies to obtain White House credentials should be greatly expanded, reducing the hold mainstream media newspapers, network television news, and cable network news have on front-row status to dominate news conferences by asking the first questions.

What must be put to an end is the ability of White House correspondents to utilize the daily press conference as an opportunity to continue the Deep State "resistance" campaign by asking a series of "gotcha" questions aimed only at developing inconsistencies and/or White House explanation shifts that can be exploited to perpetuate their "impeachment-oriented" strategy of perpetuating a hostile White House press environment. In summary, the White House counterattack against the mainstream media involves the following:

- the White House producing its own daily "Breaking News" releases attacking the Democrats and demanding an expanded Department of Justice investigation into Obama administration unmasking, the Clinton campaign "Russian collusion," and a list of other Deep State offenses

- the White House revising the rules for White House correspondents, ending daily press briefings, and moving the White House press office off-site

To win the counteroffensive on the mainstream media, the White House must take control of the news cycle, limiting the media's daily ability to attack President Trump in a cozy mainstream media–dominated press room facility located within the White House, where White House "leakers" are conveniently within reach.

Conclusion

The Fight to Save President Trump

THE DEMOCRATS, WHO HAVE supported Russia since the communist revolution in 1917, decided to explain away Hillary Clinton's devastating loss by demonizing Russia. Ironically, Hillary, who failed to become president some one hundred years after the Russian Revolution, has decided to encourage Democrats to renew the McCarthyism of the 1950s, evidently forgetting that Democrats in that time attacked Republicans backing McCarthy for making accusations without evidence, naming alleged communists that had penetrated the US State Department, the US military, and the arts, including Hollywood.

As I have stressed throughout this book, Bill Clinton and Barack Obama both won the presidency, despite their socialist message, because both were charismatic politicians. Recalling Hillary's failure at the start of her husband's presidency to institute "HillaryCare," Hillary Clinton has defined for some 35 years what it looks like to be so totally lacking in charisma as to be unable to compete on the national scene. This was evidenced both by the successful challenge Barack Obama raised to Hillary's candidacy in the 2008 Democratic presidential primaries and by the challenge raised in 2016 by Bernie Sanders.

As former DNC chair Donna Brazile has made clear, the only way Hillary could beat Bernie was by hijacking the DNC and rigging the primaries in her favor. As a presidential candidate in 2016, Hillary ran on themes of class envy and race baiting. Hillary's constant berating of the top 1 percent was patently hypocritical given the avarice she and her husband have demonstrated since first stepping onto the political stage in Arkansas.

With the Clinton Foundation being run not as a charity but as a vast criminal empire, one could easily come to the conclusion that for the Clintons, there is no such thing as "enough money," such that their foundation regularly sold favors to the most corrupt third-world criminals the Clintons could find, provided these thugs had money to "donate."

As for race baiting, Hillary's identity politics turned into a demonization of "white privilege," so as to preach to "people of color" that their economic status had to do with decades of exploitation by white colonialists and imperialists. So despite demonizing Russia to explain her inadequacies as a presidential candidate, Hillary was proud to campaign on themes that are traditionally touted by the US Communist Party.

In her amplification of the left's identity politics, Hillary insisted that all Americans should be proud to elect a woman as president. Americans generally agreed, objecting only that Hillary would not be that woman. If the Democrats move hard-left in the reaction to Hillary's devastating loss, as seems to be the case with La Raza Tom Perez and Black Muslim Keith Ellison picked to head the DNC, the Democratic Party is headed to oblivion, doomed to be an insignificant political splinter party on the far-left.

Leftist professors, supported by Obama's decision to have the government subsidize all college student loans, have produced a generation of millennials with a predisposition to hate America in their embrace of socialist-provided free education, free medical care, and government-subsidized housing, backed ultimately by a tax-payer-provided annual income. Millennials falling for Bernie Sanders's promises are about to face the economic reality that forces all socialist-oriented governments to go bankrupt and turn on their followers, who continue to demand yet more free stuff.

The Deep State Broadens "Russian Collusion" to Include ExxonMobil

In July 2017, Deep State Obama loyalists in the Treasury Department's Office of Foreign Assets Control (OFAC) filed an action against ExxonMobil charging that the corporation had signed agreements with Russia that violated sanctions the United States had imposed on Russia after its interference in Crimea and Ukraine. Trump supporters interpreted the attack from within the Treasury Department on ExxonMobil as an attempt by the Deep State to discredit Trump's secretary of state Rex Tillerson, who joined the gas and oil giant in 1975 and rose to serve as chairman and CEO from 2006 to 2017.

At the center of the dispute are interactions ExxonMobil had with the Russian oil company Rosneft and with Igor Sechin. The Treasury Department asserts that ExxonMobil violated the Ukraine-related sanctions by signing with Rosneft on or about May 14, 2014, and again on or about May 23, 2014, eight different legal documents related to oil and natural gas projects in Russia that Sechin signed in his capacity as president of Rosneft. The problem is that during the Obama administration, White House and Treasury Department officials repeatedly clarified that the sanctions imposed by the US Treasury on Russia on April 28, 2014, only applied to Sechin with regard to his personal affairs and not to the various companies that Sechin managed or represented, including Rosneft. The Treasury Department press release dated April 28, 2014, that announced sanctions on Sechin named a total of 7 Russian government officials and 17 Russian businesses that were being placed under sanctions over Russia's involvement in Ukraine. On this point, the Treasury Department press release commented that "Rosneft is a state-owned company and has not been sanctioned."[1]

In filing the federal lawsuit, the attorneys for ExxonMobil argued that the company followed clear guidance from the White House and Treasury Department. When ExxonMobil signed documents with Russia, there should have been no problem involving ongoing oil and gas activities in Russia with Rosneft—a nonsanctioned entity—that were countersigned on behalf of Rosneft by Sechin in his official capacity. The ExxonMobil attorneys also noted that at the time of the signing, there was no direct US sanction regarding pursuing an oil and natural gas joint venture with Russia.

A legal memorandum on "Ukraine-Related Sanctions" published by the prestigious law firm Sullivan & Cromwell LLP, dated May 2, 2014, strongly suggests that ExxonMobil did nothing wrong, including legal agreements with Rosneft that Sechin signed as CEO.[2] "Notably, the most recent designations include Igor Sechin, the President and Management Board Chairmen of Rosneft, Russia's leading petroleum company, but do not include Rosneft itself," the Sullivan & Cromwell memo specified. A March 17, 2014, a White House Fact Sheet said, "Our current focus is to identify these individuals and target their personal assets, but not companies that they may manage on behalf of the Russian state." The position was confirmed on May 16, 2014, by a Treasury Department spokesperson, who said by way of example that BP's American CEO was permitted to participate in Rosneft board meetings with Sechin so long as the activity related to Rosneft and not Sechin's personal business.

The core issue of the ExxonMobil lawsuit is that OFAC changed the rules after giving ExxonMobil guidance in 2014. At the time, allowing Sechin to sign the Rosneft contracts did not violate any sanctions. The ExxonMobil brief in the federal District Court case reads in part as follows:

> OFAC now seeks to penalize ExxonMobil retroactively based on eight documents executed in May 2014 with Rosneft Oil Company ("Rosneft"), the Russian state-owned oil company (the "Documents"). At the time those documents were executed in 2014, Rosneft was not subject to any sanctions, and no sanctions prohibited the activities called for or reflected in those documents. Instead, the sole basis of OFAC's July 20, 2017 penalty notice (the "Penalty Notice") is that the documents were signed on behalf of Rosneft by its President and Chairman, Igor Sechin, who at the time was subject to sanctions only in his individual capacity.

An interview published by *Der Spiegel* on September 2, 2014, described Sechin as the second most powerful man in Russia, ranked second only to President Vladimir Putin in the complicated power structure in that country.[3] *Der Spiegel* reported that Sechin and Putin have known each other since the 1990s, when the two worked together in the St. Petersburg government, with Putin appointing Sechin his deputy chief of staff during Putin's first term as president, then as deputy prime minister. The article also pointed out that Rosneft controls more oil and natural gas reserves than the energy giant ExxonMobil, with Rosneft producing 4.2 million barrels of oil daily, then estimated at almost 5 percent of global consumption.

This case illustrates how quickly after Hillary Clinton's defeat that conducting legal business dealings with Russia had become suspect. How far will this go? In a reduction to the absurd, could it be used as evidence of treason that Donald Trump may have eaten at the Russian Tea Room in Manhattan or that as president,

Trump was known to enjoy Russian salad dressing? Are all who order White Russians enemies of the state because they enjoy vodka?

The point is that just as Democrats argued appropriately in the 1950s that McCarthyism had reached a level of absurdity when Senator Joe McCarthy asserted that he had a list with the names of 205 members of the State Department who were "known communists," the same can be said of the Democrats today. That McCarthy waved a piece of paper in front of the Ohio County Women's Republican Club in Wheeling, West Virginia, did not constitute credible evidence proving that his assertion was true. Over the next few weeks, the numbers fluctuated wildly, with McCarthy at times asserting that there were 57 communists in the State Department, which changed to 10 communists the next day. Finally, McCarthy never proved there was even one communist in the State Department.[4]

At present, it is not a crime for a US citizen to visit Russia, for a US business to pursue an opportunity in Russia, or for a US politician to have a discussion with a Russian politician. What Hillary Clinton and the Democrats managed to do in the aftermath of their devastating electoral loss in 2016 was make all these activities evidence of treason, even though there was no proof whatsoever that Donald Trump's campaign had colluded with Russia to cheat Hillary out of a victory that was "rightfully" hers. What the Democrats failed to understand was that the 2016 presidential election was never designated by any official body to be a coronation of Hillary Clinton, despite how much Hillary may have imagined that the presidency was her natural right to declare.

Since the fall of the Soviet Union, Western politicians and business executives have sought to develop ties with Russia, ranging from the easing of travel restrictions to the encouragement of joint-venture international business partnerships, including oil and natural gas exploration and distribution. Hillary Clinton and her followers reveal themselves as hypocrites in demonizing

Russia when globalists in the Democratic Party such as Zbigniew Brzezinski, President Jimmy Carter's former national security advisor, openly express their hopes that the United States and Russia can work more closely together. Before his death, Brzezinski expressed his belief that supporting a Europe-oriented Russia is the way to end US sanctions against Russia and "resolve the painful Ukrainian issue through mutual compromise."[5]

On October 21, 2017, left-leaning columnist Maureen Dowd asked the 93-year-old former Democratic Party president Jimmy Carter if he thought Russia "purloined" the election from Hillary. "I don't think there's any evidence that what the Russians did changed enough votes, or any votes," Carter answered her directly.[6]

Tech Giants Tell Senate Russia Did Not Influence Election

In their mad scramble to find some proof that Russia swayed the 2016 election, Hillary supporters began arguing that Russia influenced the election by posting on social media so as to detract from Hillary's campaign. For Hillary supporters, this was a result of the "wink-wink" the Trump campaign had going with Russia—namely, that one way or another, the Trump administration would benefit Russia once in office if Russia would pay to trash Hillary on social media.

At a hearing of the Subcommittee on Crime and Terrorism of the Senate Judiciary Committee on October 31, 2017, Colin Stretch, general counsel for Facebook, testified that Russian interference before and after the election accounted for a small (0.004) percentage of all news feed traffic that was negative toward Hillary Clinton. Sean Edgett, acting general counsel for Twitter, and Richard Salgado, director of law enforcement and information security for Google, agreed that the Russian interference constituted a relatively small percentage of all content on their social media websites, adding that accounts identified as being Russian controlled were terminated as quickly as they were recognized.[7] In their prepared testimonies, each of the three social media companies attempted to estimate the extent of Russian interference during the 2016 US presidential election cycle.

FACEBOOK

Facebook reported that the disinformation campaign associated with the Internet Research Agency (IRA), a Russian company located in St. Petersburg, spent approximately $100,000 on more than 3,000 Facebook and Instagram ads between June 2015 and August 2017. Facebook's analysis also showed that the IRA accounts used ads to promote the roughly 120 Facebook pages they had set up, which in turn posted more than 80,000 pieces of content between January 2015 and August 2017. Facebook estimated that 11.4 million people in the United State saw at least one of these ads between 2015 and 2017.[8]

TWITTER

Twitter identified 36,746 accounts that generated automated, election-related content and had at least one of the characteristics used to associate an account with Russia. During the relevant period, those accounts generated approximately 1.4 million automated, election-related tweets, which collectively received approximately 288 million impressions. Twitter placed those numbers in context as follows:

- The 36,746 automated accounts that we identified as Russian-linked and tweeting election-related content represent approximately one one-hundredth of a percent (0.012%) of the total accounts on Twitter at the time.

- The 1.4 million election-related Tweets that we identified through our retrospective review as generated by Russian-linked, automated accounts constituted less than three quarters of a percent (0.74%) of the overall election-related Tweets on Twitter at the time.

· Those 1.4 million Tweets received only one-third of a percent (0.33%) of impressions on election-related Tweets. In the aggregate, automated, Russian-linked, election-related Tweets consistently underperformed in terms of impressions relative to their volume on the platform.[9]

Twitter estimated that fewer than 5 percent of all 360 million accounts active during the election period were identified with a foreign nation-state actor.

GOOGLE

Google attempted to distinguish itself from the other two websites, arguing that its search algorithms do not lead to the same viral content as do Facebook and Twitter's. Google reported finding only two accounts during the election cycle that appeared to be engaged in activity associated with known or suspected government-backed entities. These two accounts spent approximately $4,700 in connection with the 2016 US presidential election.

Google also reported finding 18 channels on YouTube with approximately 1,100 videos that were uploaded by individuals who are suspected to be associated with the Russian effort to influence the US presidential election and contained political content. These videos mostly had low view counts, with just 3 percent having more than 5,000 views, constituting only 43 hours of content. This is a relatively small amount of content; in general, people watch more than a billion hours of YouTube content a day, with 400 hours of content uploaded every minute.[10]

Twitter Admits to Blocking Anti-Hillary Tweets during 2016 Campaign

In the same Senate hearing, Twitter's Sean Edgett admitted that the site employed algorithms designed to monitor hashtags critical of Hillary Clinton, including #PodestaEmails and #DNCLeaks. This admission opens the door for Congress to demand that social media giants like Twitter, Facebook, and Google/YouTube explain the full range of detection systems they used in the 2016 campaign to censor content favorable to Trump or critical of Clinton in what appears to have been an effort to influence the outcome of the election.

In the quote that follows, Edgett couched Twitter's censorship efforts as justified by citing the company's fight to keep automation and spam off the platform, but Twitter neglected to explain whether the company's detection systems were equally protective of Trump. Here is what Edgett admitted in his prepared statement:

> Before the election, we also detected and took action on activity relating to hashtags that have since been reported as manifestations of efforts to interfere with the 2016 election. For example, our automated spam detection systems helped mitigate the impact of automated Tweets promoting the #PodestaEmails hashtag, which originated with Wikileaks' publication of thousands of emails from the Clinton campaign chairman John Podesta's Gmail account.
>
> The core of the hashtag was propagated by Wikileaks, whose account sent out a series of 118 original Tweets containing variants on the hashtag #PodestaEmails referencing the daily installments of the emails released on the Wikileaks website.
>
> In the two months preceding the election, around 57,000 users posted approximately 426,000 unique Tweets containing variations of the #PodestaEmails hashtag.

Approximately one quarter (25%) of those Tweets received internal tags from our automation detection systems that hid them from searches.

As described in greater detail below, our systems detected and hid just under half (48%) of the Tweets relating to variants of another notable hashtag, #DNCLeak, which concerned the disclosure of leaked emails from the Democratic National Committee.

These steps were part of our general efforts at the time to fight automation and spam on our platform across all areas.

Also disclosed in Edgett's testimony was that Twitter, on the average, suspends the credentials of users suspected of using the website's application programming interface to post "bot-generated" automated tweets. The only example Edgett gave was the suspension of @PatrioticPepe, an account described as "automatically relaying to all Tweets from @realDonaldTrump with spam content"—an example that suggests Twitter was censoring pro-Trump tweets to find users employing automated spam-posting techniques. Was Twitter equally as rigorous in suspending the credentials of those using automated spam-posting engines to support Clinton? Edgett's testimony was silent on this point.

Saving President Trump

Why Hillary Clinton lost in 2016 has less to do with Russia and more to do with the underlying reality that the United States is more divided now than at any time since the outbreak of the Civil War in 1861. What the Democrats fail to appreciate is that the tide of public opinion in the United States is turning against the liberalism that gave birth to Lyndon B. Johnson's "Great Society" in 1964.

After decades of an ever-expanding welfare state, we have not reduced poverty. Instead, today the United States faces the dilemma of being $20 trillion in debt, with the major promises of the "Great Society" no more fulfilled today than they were in 1964. Instead, welfare programs have created fatherless minority families. Urban centers are plagued by diminishing tax bases, decaying infrastructure, youth gangs, drug addiction, and escalating crime rates. States that have been controlled for decades by the Democratic Party are increasingly facing bankruptcy. Increasing taxes in these states only drives out productive businesses and taxpaying citizens, making it even more difficult to fulfill public pension obligations, repair degrading infrastructure, and increase public aid to education and health care.

Aging populations in decaying Democratic Party–controlled cities are increasingly uncertain about how they will survive economically even if they receive Social Security benefits. Instead of addressing honestly the failure of 1960s social welfare politics, Democratic Party leaders like Barack Obama and Hillary Clinton still believe voters embrace the 1960s consensus that racial discrimination causes poverty. Proceeding on this mistaken presumption, Obama and Hillary, two Saul Alinsky "community organizing" acolytes, employed Alinsky's tactics of "rubbing raw class and race conflicts" to advance the left's socialist mission.

But rather than finding enthusiasm in the wake of Black Lives Matter and Antifa protests, Obama and Clinton were dismayed that voters saw today's dissidents not as sympathetic 1960s civil rights marchers but as violent thugs embracing nothing but political anarchy. Pursuing their open borders and unlimited immigration rights, the Democrats in 2016 were shocked to realize that the spirit of the Minuteman and Tea Party movements still persisted as voters rejected Hillary Clinton's globalist New World Order ambitions.

The nationalism that put Donald Trump in the White House is the same nationalism that led Great Britain to vote for Brexit. Sweeping Europe today is a return to national identity that marks the beginning of the end to Jean Monet's globalist view of creating a regional European Union government on the way to becoming a One World Government. Today, an increasing number of American voters are disenchanted with the hard-left's view of a New World Order utopia. President Trump's rejection of the Paris Climate Accord was applauded by voters who see the treaty as nothing more than an international scheme to redistribute income sold under the guise of a climate crisis. Additionally, millions of Americans cheered when President Trump pulled out of UNESCO, convinced that those participating in United Nations peace-keeping missions raped women and created cholera, as was proven to be the case in Haiti following the catastrophic 2010 earthquake. Add to this the well-researched evidence that the Clinton Foundation may have stolen as much as $1 billion in the Clintons' enthusiasm to scam legitimate charity donations to rebuild Haiti.

It remains to be seen whether the country will descend into a Second Civil War. But leftists in California and New York who align with minority voters in the nation's inner cities continue to demand the welfare state must expand while voters in the red "flyover" states worry the United States is going bankrupt as increasing taxes steal wealth from productive and economically successful segments of our society.

The premise of this book is that President Trump will be saved because the crux of the argument to remove him from office is founded in the corrupt politics that gave rise to Hillary Clinton's doomed presidential candidacy in 2016. But as the Democratic Party continues to support the violent extremism of movements like Black Lives Matter and Antifa, an increasing number of Americans in the "flyover" nation will cling even harder to their Bibles and their guns. Today's mainstream media is so corrupt in its partisan journalism that all Donald Trump has needed to reach the public directly has been the simplicity of a 140-word tweet.

To those Americans who continue to believe in the Constitution of our Founding Fathers, Donald Trump's presidency is the last, best hope. The Democratic Party of Hillary Clinton seems determined to champion radical groups like Black Lives Matter and Antifa in a United States of America in which the National Football League loses fans because a group of athletes kneel in protest to the playing of the national anthem.

That the hard-left hates the theme "Make America Great Again" is of little consequence to Donald Trump voters, who concluded that if Hillary Clinton followed Barack Obama into the White House, the left's utopian dream was certain to turn into Orwell's totalitarian nightmare. While it may take Trump two terms to complete the mission, there are already millions of Americans praying that God will afford him the opportunity to do so.

The story of the 2016 election is that Hillary's "deplorables" won.

The story written in the first year of Donald Trump's presidency is that those who vote for him expect to keep on winning.

Notes

Chapter 1

1 Josh Gerstein and Kyle Cheney, "Justice Department Watchdog Details Role in Sharing Anti-Trump Texts," *Politico*, Dec. 15, 2017, https://www.politico.com/story/2017/12/15/fbi-trump-texts -justice-department-ig-299569.

2 "FBI Agent Peter Strzok's Texts with Lisa Page Disparage Trump throughout Campaign," *CBS News*, Dec. 13, 2017, https://www .cbsnews.com/news/peter-strzok-lisa-page-texts-trump-idiot/.

3 Laura Jarrett, "Months-Worth of FBI Employees' Texts Dreading Trump Victory Released to Congress," *CNN*, Dec. 13, 2017, http:// www.cnn.com/2017/12/12/politics/peter-strzok-texts-released/ index.html.

4 Jake Tapper, "Source Explains Why Comey Didn't Use 'Grossly Negligent' to Describe Clinton," *CNN*, Nov. 7, 2017, http://www .cnn.com/2017/11/07/politics/james-comey-hillary-clinton -grassley/index.html.

5 Mike Levine, "Special Counsel's Russia Probe Loses Top FBI Investigator," *ABC News*, Aug. 16, 2017, http://abcnews.go.com/

Politics/special-counsels-russia-probe-loses-top-fbi-investigator/
   story?id=49249486.

6 Mike Levine and Pierre Thomas, "Robert Mueller's Russia
   Investigation Team Loses 2nd FBI Veteran," *ABC News*, Sept.
   28, 2017, http://abcnews.go.com/US/robert-muellers-russia
   -investigation-team-loses-2nd-fbi/story?id=50166109. See also
   Garrett M. Graff, "Robert Mueller Chooses His Investigatory
   Dream Team," *Wired*, June 14, 2017, https://www.wired.com/
   story/robert-mueller-special-counsel-investigation-team/.

7 James Rosen, "Mueller Aide Fired for Anti-Trump Texts Facing
   Review for Role in Clinton Email Probe," *Fox News*, Dec. 3, 2017,
   http://www.foxnews.com/politics/2017/12/03/ex-mueller-team
   -members-role-in-clinton-probe-under-review.html.

8 Delvin Barrett, "Clinton Ally Aided Campaign of FBI Official's
   Wife," *Wall Street Journal*, Oct. 24, 2016, https://www.wsj.com/
   articles/clinton-ally-aids-campaign-of-fbi-officials-wife
   -1477266114.

9 John Solomon, "FBI Gave Clinton Email Investigation 'Special'
   Status, Deputy Director's Email Shows," *The Hill*, Nov. 15, 2017,
   http://thehill.com/homenews/news/360604-fbi-gave-clinton
   -email-investigation-special-status-deputy-directors-email.

10 Max Kutner, "FBI Acting Director Andrew McCabe Also Being
   Investigated over Clinton Emails," *Newsweek*, May 10, 2017,
   http://www.newsweek.com/fbi-acting-director-andrew-mccabe
   -clinton-emails-606801.

11 James Rosen, "Top DOJ Official Demoted amid Probe of Contacts
   with Trump Dossier Firm," *Fox News*, Dec. 7, 2017, http://www
   .foxnews.com/politics/2017/12/07/top-doj-official-demoted
   -amid-probe-contacts-with-trump-dossier-firm.html.

12 Ibid.

13 Nick Giampia, "FBI Offered Christopher Steele $50k to Confirm
   Trump Dossier: Judge Napolitano," *Fox Business*, Dec. 18, 2017,
   http://www.foxbusiness.com/politics/2017/12/18/fbi-offered
   -christopher-steele-50k-to-confirm-trump-dossier-judge
   -napolitano.html.

14 Tim Hains, "Gowdy: Did Obama Justice Department Rely on
   Steele Dossier to Get FISA Warrant?" Real Clear Politics, Oct.
   29, 2017, https://www.realclearpolitics.com/video/2017/10/29/

gowdy_did_obama_justice_department_rely_on_steele_dossier
_to_get_fisa_warrant.html.

15 "Amateur License—KM4UDZ—Ohr, Nellie H.," Federal
Communications Commission, Universal Licensing Archive
System, May 23, 2016, http://wireless2.fcc.gov/UlsApp/
LicArchive/license.jsp?archive=Y&licKey=12382876.

16 "Wife of DOJ Deputy Was Fusion GPS Employee, CIA Research
Aide, and Applied for HAM Radio License Month after
Contracting MI6 Agent Christopher Steele," Conservative Tree
House, Dec. 12, 2017, https://theconservativetreehouse.com/
2017/12/12/wife-of-doj-deputy-was-fusion-gps-employee-cia
-research-aid-and-applied-for-ham-radio-license-month-after
-contracting-mi6-agent-christopher-steele/.

17 John Gibson, "Fusion GPS Admits DOJ Official's Wife Nellie
Ohr Hired to Probe Trump," *Fox News*, Dec. 13, 2017, http://
www.foxnews.com/politics/2017/12/13/fusion-gps-admits-doj
-officials-wife-nellie-ohr-hired-to-probe-trump.html.

18 Maegan Vazquez, Pamela Brown, and Laura Jarrett, "Trump's
Lawyer Wants a Special Counsel to Investigate DOJ Official with
Fusion GPS Ties," *CNN Politics*, Dec. 12, 2017, http://www.cnn
.com/2017/12/12/politics/bruce-ohr-special-counsel/index
.html.

19 John T. Picarelli, "Expert Working Group Report on International
Organized Crime," National Institute of Justice discussion paper,
June 2010, https://www.ncjrs.gov/pdffiles1/nij/230846.pdf.

20 "Nellie H. Ohr," Wilson Center, Term: Aug. 1, 1997–Oct. 1, 1997,
https://www.wilsoncenter.org/person/nellie-h-ohr.

21 "Nellie H. Ohr," Humanities and Social Sciences Online, profile
125406, n.d., https://www.h-net.org/people/person_view.php?id
=125406.

22 "Dr. Kathleen Armstrong Hauke," *Washington Post*,
obituary, Aug. 8, 2004, http://www.legacy.com/obituaries/
washingtonpost/obituary.aspx?n=kathleen-armstrong-hauke&
pid=2495108.

23 Samuel H. Baron and Cathy Frierson, *Adventures in Russian
Historical Research: Reminiscences of American Scholars from the Cold
War to the Present* (London: Taylor & Francis, 2015), 209–10.

24 Catherine Herridge, "Mueller Deputy Praised DOJ Official after
She Defied Trump Travel Ban Order: 'I Am So Proud,'" *Fox News*,

Dec. 5, 2017, http://www.foxnews.com/politics/2017/12/05/
mueller-deputy-praised-doj-official-after-defied-trump-travel
-ban-order-am-so-proud.html. See also "JW v DOJ Yates docs
Oct 17 00832 pg 4," Judicial Watch, document archive, posted
Dec. 5, 2017, https://www.judicialwatch.org/document-archive/
jw-v-doj-yates-docs-oct-17-00832-pg-4/.

25   Michael D. Shear, Mark Landler, Matt Apuzzo, and Eric
Lichtblau, "Trump Fires Acting Attorney General Who Defied
Him," *New York Times*, Jan. 30, 2017, https://www.nytimes
.com/2017/01/30/us/politics/trump-immigration-ban-memo
.html?_r=0. See also "Executive Order Protecting Nation from
Foreign Terrorist Entry into the United States," White House,
Jan. 27, 2017, https://www.whitehouse.gov/presidential-actions/
executive-order-protecting-nation-foreign-terrorist-entry-united
-states/.

26   Ibid.

27   Sidney Powell, *Licensed to Lie: Exposing Corruption in the Department
of Justice* (Dallas, TX: Brown Books, 2014), 35, 410.

Chapter 2

1   Jonathan Allen and Amie Parnes, *Shattered: Inside Hillary Clinton's
Doomed Campaign* (New York: Crown, 2017), ix.

2   "Video Shows Hillary and Bill Clinton Premature Celebration:
They Thought They Were Winning," Live Leak, Nov. 16, 2016,
https://www.liveleak.com/view?i=2ea_1479328823.

3   Jonathan Allan and Amie Parnes, "The Moment Hillary Clinton
Was Forced to Give Up Her Dream," *New York Post*, April 30, 2017,
http://nypost.com/2017/04/30/the-moment-hillary-clinton-was
-forced-to-give-up-her-dream/.

4   Allen and Parnes, *Shattered*, 387.

5   David Remnick, "An American Tragedy," *New Yorker*, Nov. 9,
2016, http://www.newyorker.com/news/news-desk/an-american
-tragedy-2.

6   Katie Reilly, "Read Hillary Clinton's Concession Speech for the
2016 Presidential Election," *Time*, Nov. 9, 2016, http://time
.com/4564480/read-hillary-clintons-concession-speech-full
-transcript/.

7   Allen and Parnes, *Shattered*, 394–96.

8 David E. Sanger and Eric Schmitt, "Spy Agency Consensus Grows That Russia Hacked D.N.C.," *New York Times*, July 26, 2016, https://www.nytimes.com/2016/07/27/us/politics/spy-agency-consensus-grows-that-russia-hacked-dnc.html?_r=1.

9 David E. Sanger and Nick Corasaniti, "D.N.C. Says Russian Hackers Penetrated Its Files, Including Dossier on Donald Trump," *New York Times*, June 14, 2016, https://www.nytimes.com/2016/06/15/us/politics/russian-hackers-dnc-trump.html?_r=0.

10 Ashley Parker and David E. Sanger, "Donald Trump Calls on Russia to Find Hillary Clinton Emails," *New York Times*, July 27, 2016, https://www.nytimes.com/2016/07/28/us/politics/donald-trump-russia-clinton-emails.html?mcubz=0.

11 Nick Gass, "Chaffetz Seeks Probe of Whether Clinton Destroyed Evidence," Politico, Sept. 6, 2016, http://www.politico.com/story/2016/09/jason-chaffetz-clinton-destroy-evidence-227767.

12 Office of the Director of National Intelligence, "Intelligence Community Assessment: Assessing Russian Activities and Intentions in Recent U.S. Elections," ICA 2017-01D, Jan. 6, 2017, https://www.dni.gov/files/documents/ICA_2017_01.pdf.

13 D. D. Guttenplan, "Welcome to the Fight: If We Withdraw into Our Grief and Abandon Those Most Threatened by Trump's Win, History Will Never Forgive Us," *Nation*, Nov. 28, 2016, https://www.thenation.com/article/welcome-to-the-fight/.

Chapter 3

1 Mike Lofgren, *The Deep State: The Fall of the Constitution and the Rise of a Shadow Government* (New York: Penguin Random House, 2016), 5.

2 Mike Lofgren, "A Shadow Government Controls America," Reader Supported News, Feb. 22, 2014, http://readersupportednews.org/opinion2/277-75/22216-a-shadow-government-controls.

3 Jerome R. Corsi, "JFK Researchers: Trump at Risk for Assassination," Infowars, March 17, 2017, https://www.infowars.com/jfk-researchers-trump-at-risk-for-assassination/.

4 Dwight D. Eisenhower, "Military-Industrial Complex Speech," Jan. 17, 1961, archived in the Avalon Project at the Lillian Goldman Law Library, Yale Law School, http://avalon.law.yale.edu/20th_century/eisenhower001.asp.

5   Aaron Kesel, "High Ranking CIA Agent Blows Whistle on the Deep State and Shadow Government," *Activist Post*, Sept. 15, 2017, https://www.activistpost.com/2017/09/high-ranking-cia -whistleblower-deep-state-shadow-government.html.

6   Peter Dale Scott, *The American Deep State: Big Money, Big Oil, and the Struggle for U.S. Democracy*, updated ed. (Lanham, MD: Rowman & Littlefield, 2017), 103.

7   Sara Carter, "Former Obama Aide Ben Rhodes Is Now a Person of Interest in the Unmasking Investigation," Circa, Aug. 1, 2017, https://www.circa.com/story/2017/08/01/former-obama-aide -ben-rhodes-now-a-person-of-interest-in-house-intelligence -committee-unmasking-investigation.

8   Manu Raju, "Exclusive: Rice Told House Investigators She Unmasked Senior Trump Officials," *CNN Politics*, Sept. 19, 2017, http://edition.cnn.com/2017/09/13/politics/susan-rice-house -investigators-unmasked-trump-officials/index.html.

9   Maggie Haberman, Matthew Rosenberg, and Glenn Thrush, "Trump, Citing No Evidence, Suggests Susan Rice Committed Crime," *New York Times*, April 5, 2017, https://www.nytimes.com/ 2017/04/05/us/politics/trump-interview-susan-rice.html.

10   Matthew Rosenberg, Adam Goldman, and Matt Apuzzo, "Top Russian Officials Discussed How to Influence Trump Aides Last Summer," *New York Times*, May 24, 2017, https://www.nytimes .com/2017/05/24/us/politics/russia-trump-manafort-flynn .html.

11   Ibid.

12   Sharon LaFraniere, Matt Apuzzo, and Adam Goldman, "With a Picked Lock and a Threatened Indictment, Mueller Sets a Tone," *New York Times*, Sept. 18, 2017, https://www.nytimes.com/2017/ 09/18/us/politics/mueller-russia-investigation.html?referer=.

Chapter 4

1   Terrence Petty and Robert Jablon, "Oregon Is Epicenter as Trump Protests Surge across Nation," Associated Press, Nov. 11, 2016.

2   Leah Sottile, Samantha Schmidt, and Brian Murphy, "Anti-Trump Protestors Take to the Streets in Many Cities for a Third Night," *Washington Post*, Nov. 12, 2016, https://www.washingtonpost .com/news/morning-mix/wp/2016/11/11/violence-erupts-in

-portland-riot-as-anti-trump-protests-continue-in-cities-across
-the-nation/?tid=a_inl&utm_term=.76ddf45f5e71.

3   Kyle Iboshi, "Most of Arrested Portland Protestors Are from
Oregon," KGW, Nov. 15, 2016, http://www.kgw.com/news/local/
more-than-half-of-arrested-anti-trump-protesters-didnt-vote/
351964445.

4   Aimee Green, "At Least Third of Arrested Anti-Trump Protestors
Didn't Vote," *Oregonian*, Nov. 15, 2016, http://www.oregonlive
.com/portland/index.ssf/2016/11/nearly_13_of_arrested_anti
-tru.html.

5   Jim Hoft, "Here's Proof That Soros Money Is Funding the Anti-
Trump Leftist Protest-Riots," *Gateway Pundit* (blog), Nov. 14,
2016, http://www.thegatewaypundit.com/2016/11/heres-proof
-soros-money-funding-anti-trump-leftist-protest-riots/.

6   Amy Chozick, "Clinton Says 'Personal Beef' by Putin Led to
Hacking Attacks," *New York Times*, Dec. 16, 2016, http://www
.nytimes.com/2016/12/16/us/politics/hillary-clinton-russia-fbi
-comey.html.

7   Lisa Lerer, "Clinton Says Putin's 'Personal Beef' Prompted
Election Hacks," Associated Press, Dec. 16, 2016.

8   "WikiLeaks Founder Assange on Hacked Podesta, DNC Emails:
'Our Source Is Not the Russian Government,'" *Fox News*, Dec. 16,
2016, http://www.foxnews.com/politics/2016/12/16/wikileaks
-founder-assange-on-hacked-podesta-dnc-emails-our-source-is
-not-russian-government.html.

9   "Full Podesta: 'Investigate What Actually Happened' with Russia
Hacking," *NBC News*, Dec. 18, 2016, http://www.nbcnews
.com/meet-the-press/video/podesta-investigate-what-actually
-happened-with-russia-836030531626. See also "Transcript:
'Meet the Press,'" *NBC News*, Dec. 28, 2016, http://www.nbcnews
.com/meet-the-press/meet-press-12-18-2016-n697546.

10 Bradford Richardson, "Peter King: CIA Doing 'Hit Job' against
Donald Trump; 'No Evidence' Russia behind Podesta Hack,"
Washington Times, Dec. 18, 2016, http://www.washingtontimes
.com/news/2016/dec/18/peter-king-cia-doing-hit-job-against
-donald-trump-/?.

11 Patrick Howley, "Sources: Clapper Discussed Using Supreme
Court Justice to Block Trump's Inauguration," Big League
Politics, Sept. 6, 2017, https://bigleaguepolitics.com/sources

-clapper-discussed-using-supreme-court-justice-block-trumps
-inauguration/.

12 "About," Hamilton Electors, n.d., http://www.hamiltonelectors
.com/about.

13 Lilly O'Donnell, "Meet the 'Hamilton Electors' Hoping for an
Electoral College Revolt," *Atlantic*, Nov. 21, 2016, http://www
.theatlantic.com/politics/archive/2016/11/meet-the-hamilton
-electors-hoping-for-an-electoral-college-revolt/508433/.

14 Alexander Hamilton, "The Mode of Electing the President,"
Federalist Papers No. 68, March 14, 1788, http://avalon.law.yale
.edu/18th_century/fed68.asp.

15 Valerie Richardson, "Electoral College Members Harassed,
Threatened in Last-Ditch Attempt to Block Trump," *Washington
Times*, Nov. 22, 2016, http://www.washingtontimes.com/news/
2016/nov/22/gop-electors-harassed-threatened-foes-maneuver
-blo/.

16 Mark Moore, "Electors Are Being Harassed, Threatened in Bid to
Stop Trump," *New York Post*, Dec. 14, 2016, http://nypost.com/
2016/12/14/electors-are-being-harassed-threatened-in-bid-to
-stop-trump/.

Chapter 5

1 Feliks Garcia, "Women's March: Madonna Said She Thought
about 'Blowing Up White House' but 'Chose Love' Instead,"
Independent, Jan. 21, 2017, http://www.independent.co.uk/news/
world/americas/madonna-blow-up-white-house-womens-march
-washington-donald-trump-president-protest-latest-a7539741
.html.

2 Tom Batchelor, "Donald Trump Responds to Women Marches
by Claiming Protesters Didn't Vote," *Independent*, Jan. 22, 2017,
http://www.independent.co.uk/news/world/americas/donald
-trump-us-president-women-marches-inauguration-protesters
-didnt-vote-tweet-twitter-a7540141.html.

3 Clare Malone, "Clinton Could Not Win Over White Women,"
FiveThirtyEight, Nov. 9, 2016, https://fivethirtyeight.com/
features/clinton-couldnt-win-over-white-women/.

4 Kelly Riddell, "George Soros Funds Ferguson Protests, Hope to
Spur Civil Action," *Washington Times*, Jan. 14, 2015, http://www

.washingtontimes.com/news/2015/jan/14/george-soros-funds
-ferguson-protests-hopes-to-spur/.

5 Ibid.

Chapter 6

1 Bradford Richardson, "Peter King: CIA Doing 'Hit Job' against
   Donald Trump; 'No Evidence' Russia behind Podesta Hack,"
   Washington Times, Dec. 18, 2016, http://www.washingtontimes
   .com/news/2016/dec/18/peter-king-cia-doing-hit-job-against
   -donald-trump-/?.

2 Helene Cooper, "Passport Files of 3 Candidates Were Pried Into,"
   New York Times, March 22, 2008, http://www.nytimes.com/2008/
   03/22/us/politics/22passport.html.

3 "Passports Probe Focuses on Worker," *Washington Times*, March 22,
   2008, http://www.washingtontimes.com/news/2008/mar/22/
   passports-probe-focuses-on-worker/.

4 United States Department of State and the Broadcasting Board of
   Governors, Office of Inspector General, Office of Audits, "Review
   of Controls and Notification for Access to Passport Records
   in the Department of State's Passport Information Electronic
   Records System (PIERS)," AID/IP-08-9, July 2008.

5 Ken Timmerman, "Obama's Intelligence Adviser Involved in
   Security Breach," NewsMax, Jan. 12, 2009, http://www.newsmax
   .com/KenTimmerman/brennan-passport-breach/2009/01/12/
   id/337482.

6 Jerome R. Corsi, "Brennan: Don't Use 'Jihad' to Describe
   Terrorists," WND, Jan. 9, 2013, http://www.wnd.com/2013/01/
   brennan-dont-use-jihad-to-describe-terrorists/. See also "John
   Brennan Speaks on National Security at NYU," YouTube video,
   posted by "The Obama White House," Feb. 13, 2010, https://www
   .youtube.com/watch?v=mKUpmFb4h_U&NR=1.

7 "James Clapper: Still No Evidence of Any Russian Collusion with
   Trump Campaign," *Washington Examiner*, May 8, 2017, http://
   www.washingtonexaminer.com/james-clapper-still-no-evidence
   -of-any-russian-collusion-with-trump-campaign/article/
   2622452.

8 "Gowdy Grills Brennan: Do You Have Evidence of Trump-Russia
   Collusion or Not? Brennan: 'I Don't Do Evidence,'" Real Clear
   Politics, May 23, 2017, https://www.realclearpolitics.com/

video/2017/05/23/gowdy_grills_john_brennan_do_you_have
_evidence_of_trump-russia_collusion_or_not_brennan_i_dont
_do_evidence.html.

9 Jordan Fabian, "Sessions Recuses Himself from Russia
Probe," *Hill*, March 2, 2017, http://thehill.com/homenews/
administration/322069-sessions-recuses-himself-from-russia
-probe.

10 Michael D. Shear and Matt Apuzzo, "F.B.I. Director James Comey
Is Fired by Trump," *New York Times*, May 9, 2017, https://www
.nytimes.com/2017/05/09/us/politics/james-comey-fired-fbi
.html?mcubz=0&_r=0.

11 Dave Boyer, "Trump Made Right Call in Firing Flynn, White
House Says," *Washington Times*, April 27, 2017, http://www
.washingtontimes.com/news/2017/apr/27/white-house-trump
-made-right-call-firing-flynn/.

12 "Rod Rosenstein's Letter Appointing Mueller Special Counsel,"
New York Times, May 17, 2017, https://www.nytimes.com/
interactive/2017/05/17/us/politics/document-Robert-Mueller
-Special-Counsel-Russia.html?mcubz=0.

13 Dakshayani Shankar, "Rod Rosenstein: What to Know about the
Deputy Attorney General under Sessions," *ABC News*, July 26,
2017, http://abcnews.go.com/Politics/rod-rosenstein-deputy
-attorney-general-sessions/story?id=48845480.

14 "Judicial Watch Releases Independent Counsel Memo Laying
Out Criminal Case against Hillary Clinton in Whitewater Land
Scandal," Judicial Watch, Jan. 28, 2016, http://www.judicialwatch
.org/press-room/press-releases/judicial-watch-releases-office
-of-independent-counsel-oic-memoranda-laying-out-criminal
-case-against-hillary-clinton-in-whitewatercastle-grande-land
-scandal/.

15 Teresa Welsh, "Push to Unseal the Draft Whitewater Indictment
against Hillary Clinton Gets Court Date," *State*, Sept. 20,
2017, http://www.thestate.com/news/politics-government/
article174456711.html.

16 Maryalice Parks, Erin Dooley, Mike Levine, and Adam Kelsey,
"James Comey: Everything You Need to Know about the Former
FBI Director," *ABC News*, June 6, 2017, http://abcnews.go.com/
Politics/james-comey-fired-fbi-director/story?id=40361245.

17 Josh Gerstein, "Comey 'Enthusiastic' about Bill Clinton Probe in 2001, FBI Memo Says," Politico, Jan. 18, 2017, http://www.politico.com/story/2017/01/james-comey-fbi-bill-clinton-233808.

18 "Sandy Berger Probed over Terror Memos," *Fox News*, July 20, 2004, http://www.foxnews.com/story/2004/07/20/sandy-berger-probed-over-terror-memos.html.

19 "Convicted Document Thief Sandy Berger Secretly Worked for Hillary Clinton Campaign," Conservative Base, Nov. 16, 2016, https://conservativebase.com/convicted-document-thief-sandy-berger-secretly-worked-for-hillary-clinton-campaign/.

20 "HSBC Bank Says Comey Resigns from Board to Head FBI," *Daily Star*, Aug. 1, 2013, http://www.thedailystar.net/news/hsbc-bank-says-comey-resigns-from-board-to-head-fbi.

21 Aruna Viswanatha and Brett Wolf, "HSBC to Pay $1.9 Billion U.S. Fine in Money-Laundering Case," Reuters, Dec. 11, 2012, http://www.reuters.com/article/us-hsbc-probe/hsbc-to-pay-1-9-billion-u-s-fine-in-money-laundering-case-idUSBRE8BA05M20121211.

22 Senate Homeland Security and Governmental Affairs, Permanent Subcommittee on Investigations, "HSBC Exposed U.S. Financial System to Money Laundering, Drug, Terrorist Financing Risks," HSGAC Senate, July 16, 2012, https://www.hsgac.senate.gov/subcommittees/investigations/media/hsbc-exposed-us-finacial-system-to-money-laundering-drug-terrorist-financing-risks.

23 "Quarterly Report to the United States Congress," Special Inspector General for Afghanistan Reconstruction (SIGAR), April 30, 2017, https://www.sigar.mil/pdf/quarterlyreports/2017-04-30qr.pdf.

24 Barbara Crossette, "Taliban's Ban on Poppy a Success, U.S. Aides Say," *New York Times*, May 20, 2001, http://www.nytimes.com/2001/05/20/world/taliban-s-ban-on-poppy-a-success-us-aides-say.html?mcubz=0.

25 Patrick Howley, "James Comey's Brother Works for the Law Firm That Does the Clinton Foundation Taxes," Big League Politics, May 12, 2017, https://bigleaguepolitics.com/james-comeys-brother-works-law-firm-clinton-foundations-taxes/.

26 Nate Raymond, "Clintons' Tax Man Is a Hogan & Hartson Partner," *American Lawyer*, April 8, 2008, http://www.americanlawyer.com/id=900005561221/Clintons-Tax-Man-Is-a

-Hogan-Hartson-Partner?slreturn=20170903150158. On May 1, 2010, Hogan Lovells was formed when Washington-based Hogan & Hartson merged with the London-based law firm Lovells.

27 Hank Berrien, "Loretta Lynch Has Private Meeting with Bill Clinton. What Did They Talk About?" *Daily Wire*, June 29, 2016, https://www.dailywire.com/news/7069/loretta-lynch-has-private -meeting-bill-clinton-hank-berrien.

28 Peter Schweizer, *Clinton Cash: The Untold Story of How and Why Foreign Governments and Businesses Helped Make Bill and Hillary Rich* (New York: Harper, 2015), chapter 2, "The Transfer: Bill's Excellent Kazakh Adventure," 21–37, and chapter 3, "Hillary's Reset: The Russian Uranium Deal," 39–57.

29 David Jackson and Maureen Groppe, "After Attacking AG Jeff Sessions for Failing to Investigate Hillary Clinton, Trump Won't Say If He Will Fire Him," *USA Today*, July 25, 2017, https://www.usatoday.com/story/news/politics/2017/07/25/ trump-attacks-jeff-sessions-failing-investigate-hillary-clinton/ 507568001/.

30 Jen Lawrence, "Robert Creamer Visited Obama's White House 340 Times," Breitbart, Oct. 19, 2016, http://www.breitbart.com/big -government/2016/10/19/robert-creamer-okeefe-investigation -fame-visited-obamas-whitehouse-340-times/.

31 Valerie Richardson, "Democratic Heads Roll after Video Shows Agitators Planted at Trump Rallies," *Washington Times*, Oct. 18, 2016, http://www.washingtontimes.com/news/2016/oct/18/ undercover-video-shows-democrats-saying-they-hire-/.

32 "Trump DOJ: No Plans to Charge Lois Lerner in IRS Scandal," *Fox News*, Sept. 8, 2017, http://www.foxnews.com/politics/2017/ 09/08/doj-declines-to-charge-lois-lerner-in-irs-scandal.html.

Chapter 7

1 US Senate Select Committee to Study Governmental Operations with respect to Intelligence Activities, *Book II: Intelligence Activities and the Rights of Americans* (Washington, DC: US Government Printing Office, 1976), 4. This is the final report of what has come to be known as the "Church Committee," named after the chairman of the Select Committee, Senator Frank Church (Democrat, Idaho).

2   "Edward Snowden: Leaks That Exposed U.S. Spy Programme,"
    BBC News, Jan. 17, 2014, http://www.bbc.com/news/world-us
    -canada-23123964.

3   Ashley Gorski and Patrick Toomey, "Unprecedented and
    Unlawful: The NSA 'Upstream' Surveillance," ACLU, Sept. 23,
    2016, https://www.aclu.org/blog/national-security/privacy
    -and-surveillance/unprecedented-and-unlawful-nsas-upstream
    ?redirect=blog/speak-freely/unprecedented-and-unlawful-nsas
    -upstream-surveillance.

4   John Solomon, "Newly Declassified Memos Detail Extent of
    Improper Obama-Era NSA Spying," *Hill,* July 25, 2017, http://
    thehill.com/policy/national-security/343785-newly-declassified
    -memos-detail-extent-of-improper-obama-era-nsa.

5   Sara A. Carter, "Obama Intel Agency Secretly Conducted Illegal
    Searches on Americans for Years," Circa, May 23, 2017, https://
    www.circa.com/story/2017/05/23/politics/obama-intel-agency
    -secretly-conducted-illegal-searches-on-americans-for-years.

6   Anthony Loewenstein, "The Ultimate Goal of the NSA Is Total
    Population Control," *Guardian,* July 10, 2014, https://www
    .theguardian.com/commentisfree/2014/jul/11/the-ultimate
    -goal-of-the-nsa-is-total-population-control.

7   Barton Gellman and Ashkan Soltani, "NSA Surveillance
    Program Reaches 'into the Past' to Retrieve, Replay Phone Calls,"
    Washington Post, March 18, 2014, https://www.washingtonpost
    .com/world/national-security/nsa-surveillance-program-reaches
    -into-the-past-to-retrieve-replay-phone-calls/2014/03/18/
    226d2646-ade9-11e3-a49e-7badc9210f19_story.html?utm_term
    =.63c31f5b9966.

8   Ibid.

9   Glenn Greenwald, "NSA Collecting Phone Records of Millions
    of Verizon Customers Daily," *Guardian,* June 6, 2013, https://
    www.theguardian.com/world/2013/jun/06/nsa-phone-records
    -verizon-court-order.

10 Joshua Caplan, "Roger Stone Says He Knows the Wall Street
    Billionaire behind 'Trump Dossier,'" *Gateway Pundit* (blog), Oct.
    26, 2017, http://www.thegatewaypundit.com/2017/10/roger
    -stone-says-knows-wall-street-billionaire-behind-trump-dossier
    -video/. Also see Kenneth P. Vogel and Maggie Haberman,
    "Conservative Website First Funded Anti-Trump Research by

Firm That Later Produced Dossier," *New York Times*, Oct. 27, 2017, https://www.nytimes.com/2017/10/27/us/politics/trump -dossier-paul-singer.html.

11   Adam Entous, Devlin Barrett, and Rosalind S. Helderman, "Clinton Campaign, DNC Paid for Research That Led to Russia Dossier," *Washington Post*, Oct. 24, 2017, https://www .washingtonpost.com/world/national-security/clinton -campaign-dnc-paid-for-research-that-led-to-russia-dossier/ 2017/10/24/226fabf0-b8e4-11e7-a908-a3470754bbb9_story.html ?utm_term=.57eacdfe98b8.

12   "Fusion GPS Fallout: DNC, Clinton, FBI Take Heat after Bombshell That Dems Funded Trump Dossier," *Fox News*, Oct. 25, 2017, http://www.foxnews.com/politics/2017/10/25/fusion -gps-fallout-dnc-clinton-fbi-take-heat-after-bombshell-that -dems-funded-trump-dossier.html.

13   "Perkins Coie Got Obama's Birth Certificate," *BLT* (blog), *Legal Times*, April 27, 2011, http://legaltimes.typepad.com/blt/2011/ 04/perkins-coie-judith-corley-got-obamas-birth-certificate.html.

14   Jerome R. Corsi, "Look Who's Married to Obama's Media 'Controller,'" WND, Oct. 20, 2009, http://www.wnd.com/2009/ 10/113562/.

15   Sean Davis, "Obama's Campaign Paid $972,000 to Law Firm That Secretly Paid Fusion GPS in 2016," *Federalist*, Oct. 29, 2017, http://thefederalist.com/2017/10/29/obamas -campaign-gave-972000-law-firm-funneled-money-fusion-gps/ #.WfVnoH-5PM0.twitter.

16   David Corn, "A Veteran Spy Has Given the FBI Information Alleging a Russian Operation to Cultivate Donald Trump," *Mother Jones*, Oct. 31, 2016, http://www.motherjones.com/ politics/2016/10/veteran-spy-gave-fbi-info-alleging-russian -operation-cultivate-donald-trump/.

17   Tom Hamburger and Rosalind S. Helderman, "FBI Once Planned to Pay Former British Spy Who Authored Controversial Trump Dossier," *Washington Post*, Feb. 28, 2017, https://www .washingtonpost.com/politics/fbi-once-planned-to-pay-former -british-spy-who-authored-controversial-trump-dossier/2017/ 02/28/896ab470-facc-11e6-9845-576c69081518_story.html?utm _term=.47e466b489fc.

18 Letter from Senate Minority Leader Harry Reid, addressed to James Comey, director of the FBI, Oct. 30, 2016, http://static .politico.com/2e/1a/5bb86d684289bd506452c43b1065/reid -letter-to-comey.pdf.

19 Ken Bensinger, Miriam Elder, and Mark Schoofs, "These Reports Allege Trump Has Deep Ties to Russia," BuzzFeed, Jan. 10, 2017, https://www.buzzfeed.com/kenbensinger/these-reports -allege-trump-has-deep-ties-to-russia?utm_term=.clnE9oeA73 #.ikvEvq4lyw. The same day, BuzzFeed published the Christopher Steele–authored Fusion GPS "Russia dossier" on Trump on the internet, https://www.documentcloud.org/documents/3259984 -Trump-Intelligence-Allegations.html.

20 Robert Gilette, "My Turn: Inside the Trump Dossier," *Concord Monitor*, Jan. 27, 2017, http://www.concordmonitor.com/Trump -and-the-Russia-connection-part-one-7646273.

21 Ibid.

22 Director of national intelligence, "Background to 'Assessing Russian Activities and Intentions in Recent U.S. Elections': The Analytic Process and Cyber Incident Attribution," DNI, Jan. 6, 2017, https://www.dni.gov/files/documents/ICA_2017_01.pdf.

23 Julian Borger, "The Trump-Russia Dossier: Why Its Findings Grow More Significant by the Day," *Guardian*, Oct. 7, 2017, https://www.theguardian.com/us-news/2017/oct/07/trump -russia-steele-dossier-moscow.

24 Letter from Matthew J. Gehringer, general counsel, Perkins Coie LLP, published by the *Washington Post*, Oct. 24, 2017, https://www .documentcloud.org/documents/4116755-PerkinsCoie-Fusion -PrivilegeLetter-102417.html.

25 "Bryon York: FBI Fights Public Release of Trump Dossier Info," *Washington Examiner*, Aug. 31, 2017, http://www .washingtonexaminer.com/byron-york-fbi-fights-public-release -of-trump-dossier-info/article/2633048. See also Patrick J. Buchanan, "The Other Plot—to Bring Down Trump," WND, Oct. 30, 2017, http://www.wnd.com/2017/10/that-other-plot-to-bring -down-trump/.

26 David A. Fahrenthold, "Trump Recording Having Extremely Lewd Conversations about Women In 2015," *Washington Post*, Oct. 8, 2016, https://www.washingtonpost.com/politics/trump -recorded-having-extremely-lewd-conversation-about-women

-in-2005/2016/10/07/3b9ce776-8cb4-11e6-bf8a-3d26847eeed4
_story.html?utm_term=.49dd31b4905b.

27 Kyle Cheney and Sarah Wheaton, "The Most Revealing Clinton
Campaign Emails in WikiLeaks Release," Politico, Oct. 7,
2017, https://www.politico.com/story/2016/10/john-podesta
-wikileaks-hacked-emails-229304.

28 "Julian Assange on Seth Rich," YouTube video, posted by
"Nieuwsuur," Aug. 9, 2016, https://www.youtube.com/watch?v=
Kp7FkLBRpKg.

29 Michelle Ye Hee Lee, "Julian Assange's Claim That There Was No
Russian Involvement in WikiLeaks Emails," *Washington Post*, Jan. 5,
2017, https://www.washingtonpost.com/news/fact-checker/wp/
2017/01/05/julian-assanges-claim-that-there-was-no-russian
-involvement-in-wikileaks-emails/?utm_term=.25019330a718.

30 Patrick Lawrence, "A New Report Raises Big Questions about Last
Year's DNC Hack," *Nation*, Aug. 9, 2017, https://www.thenation
.com/article/a-new-report-raises-big-questions-about-last-years
-dnc-hack/.

31 "Intel Vets Challenge 'Russia Hack' Evidence," *Consortium News*,
July 24, 2017, https://consortiumnews.com/2017/07/24/intel
-vets-challenge-russia-hack-evidence/.

32 Chuck Ross, "Mueller Picks Another Clinton/Obama Donor for
Russia Probe Team," *Daily Caller*, Sept. 16, 2017, http://dailycaller
.com/2017/09/16/mueller-picks-another-clintonobama-donor
-for-russia-probe-team/.

33 Josh Siegel, "Trump Questions Mueller's Investigation: It's Full of
'Hillary Supporters,'" *Washington Examiner*, June 22, 2017, http://
www.washingtonexaminer.com/trump-questions-muellers
-investigation-its-full-of-hillary-clinton-supporters/article/
2626883.

34 Evan Perez, Shimon Prokupecz, and Pamela Brown, "Exclusive:
U.S. Government Wiretapped Former Trump Campaign
Chairman," *CNN Politics*, Sept. 19, 2017, http://www.cnn.com/
2017/09/18/politics/paul-manafort-government-wiretapped-fisa
-russians/index.html.

35 Jerome R. Corsi, "FBI Director Silent on Whether Anti-Trump
Agent Used Peegate Dossier to Greenlight Trump Spying,"
Infowars, Dec. 7, 2017, https://www.infowars.com/fbi-director

-silent-on-whether-anti-trump-agent-used-peegate-dossier-to
-greenlight-trump-spying/.

Chapter 8

1 "Uranium and Nuclear Power in Kazakhstan," World Nuclear
   Association, updated August 2017, http://www.world-nuclear
   .org/information-library/country-profiles/countries-g-n/
   kazakhstan.aspx.

2 Andrew McCarthy, "Clinton's State Department: A RICO
   Enterprise," *National Review*, Oct. 29, 2016, http://www
   .nationalreview.com/article/441573/hillary-clinton-corruption
   -foundation-was-key.

3 Jo Becker and Don Van Natta Jr., "After Mining Deal, Financier
   Donated to Clinton," *New York Times*, Jan. 31, 2008, http://www
   .nytimes.com/2007/01/25/world/europe/25nuke.html.

4 Andrew C. McCarthy, "The Obama Administration's Uranium
   One Scandal," *National Review*, Oct. 21, 2017, http://www
   .nationalreview.com/article/452972/uranium-one-deal-obama
   -administration-doj-hillary-clinton-racketeering. The account of
   Tenem USA and the Russian spy scheme to bribe the Clintons is
   drawn from this source.

5 Isabel Gorst, "Former Kazakh Nuclear Chief Given Jail Term,"
   Financial Times, March 12, 2010, https://www.ft.com/content/
   965ba1f2-2dfc-11df-b85c-00144feabdc0?mhq5j=e6.

6 Andrew C. McCarthy, "Uranium One Focus: Corruption, Not
   National Security," *National Review*, Nov. 15, 2017, http://www
   .nationalreview.com/corner/453758/unranium-one-focus
   -corruption-not-national-security.

7 Ibid.

8 John Solomon and Alison Spann, "FBI Uncovered Russian
   Bribery Plot before Obama Administration Approved
   Controversial Nuclear Deal with Moscow," *Hill*, Oct. 17, 2017,
   http://thehill.com/policy/national-security/355749-fbi
   -uncovered-russian-bribery-plot-before-obama-administration.

9 "Kazakhstan: Economic and Energy Update, June 7–20," State
   Department memorandum, June 28, 2009, released by WikiLeaks,
   https://search.wikileaks.org/plusd/cables/09ASTANA1088_a
   .html.

10 David Krayden, "Emails Connect Hillary with Uranium One Player—'All I Can to Support Secretary Clinton,'" *Daily Caller*, Oct. 14, 2016, http://dailycaller.com/2016/10/14/e-mails-connect-hillary-with-uranium-one-player-all-i-can-to-support-secretary-clinton/.

11 Peter Koven, "Uranium One Bought by Top Russian Shareholder ARMZ for $1.3 billion," *Financial Post*, Jan. 14, 2013, http://business.financialpost.com/commodities/mining/uranium-one-bought-by-top-russian-shareholder-armz-for-1-3-billion.

12 Wilson Andrews, "Donations to the Clinton Foundation, and a Russian Takeover," *New York Times*, April 22, 2015, https://www.nytimes.com/interactive/2015/04/23/us/clinton-foundation-donations-uranium-investors.html?_r=0.

13 Peter Schweizer, "Trump Vs. Clintons' Russia Ties (Guess Who Got a Free Pass)," *Fox News*, March 3, 2017, http://www.foxnews.com/opinion/2017/03/03/peter-schweizer-trump-vs-clintons-russia-ties-guess-who-always-got-free-pass.html.

14 John Solomon and Alison Spann, "Uranium One Deal Led to Some Exports to Europe, Memos Show," *Hill*, Nov. 2, 2017, http://thehill.com/policy/national-security/358339-uranium-one-deal-led-to-some-exports-to-europe-memos-show.

15 Sara A. Carter, "A Russian Nuclear Firm under FBI Investigation Was Allowed to Purchase U.S. Uranium Supply," Circa, Oct. 17, 2017, https://www.circa.com/story/2017/10/17/national-security/the-fbi-uncovered-russian-nuclear-kickback-scheme-months-before-the-obama-administration-passed-uranium-one-deal-with-moscow.

16 "Alerting GOR of Delivery of Seized HEU during September 21 Director's Trip to Moscow," secret cable, Aug. 17, 2009, released by WikiLeaks, https://wikileaks.org/plusd/cables/09STATE85588_a.html.

17 Shephard Ambellas, "Hillary Clinton Requested FBI Mueller Deliver Highly Enriched Uranium to the Russians in 2009 in Secret 'Plane-Side Tarmac Meeting,'" Intelhub, June 19, 2017, https://www.intellihub.com/hillary-clinton-requested-fbi-dir-mueller-deliver-highly-enriched-uranium-russians/.

18 See "Kazakhstan: Kazatomprom Plays Lead Role in Country's Uranium Production Ambitions," State Department cable, Nov. 10, 2008, released by WikiLeaks, https://search.wikileaks

.org/plusd/cables/08ASTANA2232_a.html; "Kazakhstan's Uranium Market: Key Players, Plans, and Prospects," State Department cable, Feb. 4, 2009, released by WikiLeaks, https://search.wikileaks.org/plusd/cables/09ASTANA209_a.html; and "Kazakhstan: Economic and Energy Update, April 16–May 9," State Department cable, May 18, 2009, released by WikiLeaks, https://search.wikileaks.org/plusd/cables/09ASTANA855_a.html.

19 "Did Hillary Clinton Tell FBI's Mueller to Deliver Uranium to Russians in 2009 'Secret Tarmac Meeting'?," Snopes, June 21, 2017, https://www.snopes.com/hillary-clinton-robert-mueller-uranium/.

20 "Lobbyists Representing Uranium One, 2010–2015," Open Secrets, n.d., https://www.opensecrets.org/lobby/clientlbs.php?id=D000065156&year=2015.

21 John R. Schindler, "Panama Papers Reveal Clinton's Kremlin Connection: John and Tony Podesta Aren't Fooling Anyone," Observer, April 7, 2016, http://observer.com/2016/04/panama-papers-reveal-clintons-kremlin-connection/.

22 Ibid.

23 Peter Hobson, "Ukraine Charges Russia's Sberbank with 'Financial Terrorism,'" *Moscow Times*, April 17, 2014, https://themoscowtimes.com/articles/ukraine-charges-russias-sberbank-with-financing-terrorism-34125.

24 Lachlan Markay, "'Panama Papers' Implicate Client of Clinton-Linked Lobbying Firm," *Washington Free Beacon*, April 5, 2016, http://freebeacon.com/issues/panama-papers-implicate-podesta-client/.

25 Roman Anin, Olesya Shmagun, and Dmitry Velikovsky, "Panama Papers: The Secret Caretaker," Organized Crime and Corruption Reporting Project (OCCRP), April 3, 2016, https://www.occrp.org/en/panamapapers/the-secret-caretaker/.

26 Isaac Arnsdorf, "Etsy Registers," Politico, March 30, 2016, http://www.politico.com/tipsheets/politico-influence/2016/03/etsy-registers-podesta-for-sberbank-lend-lease-cov-for-bacardi-livingston-for-curacao-and-st-maarten-pizza-for-hillary-213495.

27 Nicholas Confessore and Amy Chozick, "Unease at Clinton Foundation over Finances and Ambitions," *New York Times*,

Aug. 13, 2013, http://www.nytimes.com/2013/08/14/us/politics/
unease-at-clinton-foundation-over-finances-and-ambitions.html
?hp&_r=1&&pagewanted=all.

28 "The Panama Papers: Politicians, Criminals and the Rogue
Industry That Hides Their Cash," International Consortium of
Investigative Journalists (ICIJ), 2017, https://panamapapers.icij
.org.

29 Peter Schweizer, "The Clinton Foundation, State and Kremlin
Connections," *Wall Street Journal*, July 31, 2016, https://www
.wsj.com/articles/the-clinton-foundation-state-and-kremlin
-connections-1469997195. Subsequent paragraphs are drawn
from this source.

30 "State in 70 Million Euro Aids Partnership in Africa," *Irish
Times*, Oct. 26, 2006, https://www.wsj.com/articles/the-clinton
-foundation-state-and-kremlin-connections-1469997195.

31 Sarah Westwood, "Emails Show Clinton Ties to Russian Oligarch
under Investigation," *Washington Examiner*, Sept. 12, 2016,
http://www.washingtonexaminer.com/emails-show-clinton
-ties-to-russian-oligarch-under-investigation/article/2601514.
Subsequent paragraphs are drawn from this source.

32 "From Russia with Money: Hillary Clinton, the Russian Reset,
and Cronyism," Government Accountability Institute, 2016,
http://www.g-a-i.org/wp-content/uploads/2016/08/Report
-Skolkvovo-08012016.pdf.

33 Stephen K. Bannon and Peter Schweizer, "Report: Hillary
Clinton's Campaign Manager John Podesta Sat on Board of
Company That Bagged $35 Million from Putin-Connected
Russian Government Fund," Breitbart, Aug. 1, 2016, http://www
.breitbart.com/2016-presidential-race/2016/08/01/report-hillary
-clintons-campaign-mgr-john-podesta-sat-board-company
-bagged-35-million-putin-connected-russian-govt-fund-2/.

34 Jerome R. Corsi, "How Hillary's Campaign Chief Hid Money from
Russia," WND, Oct. 17, 2016, http://www.wnd.com/2016/10/
how-hillarys-campaign-chief-hid-money-from-russia/.

35 "'Fwd: Podesta Outstanding Docs for Joule,' Email #4635
Released by WikiLeaks in Podesta DNC Emails," email dated
Jan. 7, 2014, https://wikileaks.org/podesta-emails/emailid/4635.

36 Mark Hosenball and Warren Strobel, "With Cash, Ukraine's
Political Foes Bring Fight to Washington," Reuters, Dec. 20, 2013,

https://www.reuters.com/article/us-usa-ukraine-lobbying/
with-cash-ukraines-political-foes-bring-fight-to-washington
-idUSBRE9BJ1B220131220.

37 "Putin: Russia Helped Yanukovych to Flee Ukraine," *BBC
    News*, Oct. 24, 2014, http://www.bbc.com/news/world-europe
    -29761799.

38 "Ukraine: Extreme Makeover for the Party of Regions," State
    Department memo, Feb. 3, 2006, released by WikiLeaks, https://
    wikileaks.org/plusd/cables/06KIEV473_a.html.

39 Gabrielle Levy, "Ukraine Documents Detail Cash Payments to
    Paul Manafort," *U.S. News*, Aug. 15, 2016, https://www.usnews
    .com/news/articles/2016-08-15/ukraine-documents-detail-cash
    -payments-to-paul-manafort.

40 Andrew E. Kramer, Mike McIntire, and Barry Meier, "Secret
    Ledger in Ukraine Lists Cash for Donald Trump's Campaign
    Chief," *New York Times*, Aug. 14, 2016, https://www.nytimes.com/
    2016/08/15/us/politics/paul-manafort-ukraine-donald-trump
    .html?_r=2.

41 Emily Zanotti, "Special Counsel Robert Mueller Now
    Investigating Tony Podesta, Podesta Group in Russia Probe,"
    Daily Wire, Oct. 23, 2017, http://www.dailywire.com/news/
    22614/special-counsel-robert-mueller-now-investigating-emily
    -zanotti.

Chapter 9

1 "The Top Watchdog against Fake News and Propaganda:
   Transforming the Media Landscape," Media Matters, privately
   distributed donor briefing book, "Media Matters for America
   2020 Plan," privately published.

2 Nick Wingfield, Mike Isaac, and Katie Benner, "Google and
   Facebook Take Aim at Fake News Sites," *New York Times*, Nov. 14,
   2017, https://www.nytimes.com/2016/11/15/technology/google
   -will-ban-websites-that-host-fake-news-from-using-its-ad-service
   .html?_r=1.

3 Tess Townsend, "Google Has Banned 200 Publishers since It
   Passed a New Policy against Fake News," Recode, Jan 25, 2017,
   https://www.recode.net/2017/1/25/14375750/google-adsense
   -advertisers-publishers-fake-news.

4 Bill Vandenberg, "Democracy Fund, April 6, 2012 Docket, Open Society Foundation," memorandum to Aryeh Neier and Diana Morris, retrieved March 27, 2012, http://www.fbcoverup .com/docs/library/2012-03-27-Democracy-Fund-Apr-06-2012 -Bill-Vandenberg-on-ousting-of-Glen-Beck-from-Fox-and-Pat -Buchanan-from-MSNBC-Soros-Open-Society-Foundations -DCLeaks-Mar-27-2012.pdf.

5 "Our Mission," Color of Change, n.d., https://www.colorofchange .org/about/.

6 Jack Mirkinson, "Glenn Beck's Last Fox News Show: Recap of the Finale," *Huffington Post*, Aug. 30, 2011, https://www .huffingtonpost.com/2011/06/30/glenn-beck-fox-news-last-show _n_888155.html.

7 Tim Mak, "Pat Buchanan Axed by MSNBC," Politico, Feb. 17, 2012, http://www.politico.com/story/2012/02/msnbc-axes -pat-buchanan-073014; and Patrick J. Buchanan, *Suicide of a Superpower: Will America Survive to 2025?* (New York: St. Martin's, 2011).

8 Patrick J. Buchanan, "Blacklisted, but Not Beaten," *American Conservative*, Feb. 16, 2012, http://www.theamericanconservative .com/2012/02/16/blacklisted-but-not-beaten/.

9 "Forcing the Glenn Beck Show off Fox News," Color of Change, n.d., https://colorofchange.org/campaigns/victories/glennbeck/.

10 "Call on CNN to Fire Lou Dobbs," Color of Change, n.d., https://colorofchange.org/campaigns/past/fire-lou-dobbs/. The language quoted here has been removed from the Color of Change website at https://www.colorofchange.org/dobbs/. See also Jerome R. Corsi, "Lou Dobbs Targeted by Leftist Scheme," WND, Sept. 7, 2016, http://www.wnd.com/2016/09/major -network-anchor-targeted-by-left/.

11 "Lou Dobbs Quits CNN in Surprise Announcement," Fox News Entertainment, Nov. 11, 2009, http://www.foxnews.com/ entertainment/2009/11/11/report-lou-dobbs-leave-cnn.html.

12 Emily Steel and Michael S. Schmidt, "Bill O'Reilly Thrives at Fox News, Even as Harassment Settlements Add Up," *New York Times*, April 1, 2017, https://www.nytimes.com/2017/04/01/business/ media/bill-oreilly-sexual-harassment-fox-news.html?_r=1text -decoration:none.

13 Media Matters Staff, "These Are Bill O'Reilly's Advertisers," Media Matters, April 4, 2017, https://www.mediamatters.org/blog/2017/04/04/these-are-bill-o-reilly-s-advertisers-oreilly-factor/215912.

14 "Indivisible: The Guide," available for download at https://www.indivisible.org/guide/.

15 Fred Lucas, "'Indivisible,' with Ties to George Soros, Sows Division among GOP Lawmakers," *Daily Signal*, Feb. 10, 2017, http://dailysignal.com/2017/02/10/indivisible-with-ties-to-george-soros-sows-division-against-trump-gop-lawmakers/.

16 Aaron Bandler, "7 Things You Need to Know about the Healthcare Town Hall Protesters," *Daily Wire*, Feb. 22, 2017, http://www.dailywire.com/news/13745/7-things-you-need-know-about-healthcare-town-hall-aaron-bandler.

Chapter 10

1 "Anarchist Extremists: Antifa," State of New Jersey, Department of Homeland Security and Preparedness, June 12, 2017, https://www.njhomelandsecurity.gov/analysis/anarchist-extremists-antifa?rq=antifa.

2 Josh Meyer, "FBI, Homeland Security Warn of More 'Antifa' Attacks," Politico, Sept. 1, 2017, http://www.politico.com/story/2017/09/01/antifa-charlottesville-violence-fbi-242235.

3 Tyler Durden, "FBI, DHS Officially Classify Antifa Activities as 'Domestic Terrorist Violence," Zero Hedge, Sept. 1, 2017, http://www.zerohedge.com/news/2017-09-01/fbi-dhs-study-reveals-antifa-primary-instigators-violence-public-rallies-april-2016.

4 This quotation and the previous three paragraphs are drawn from Tom Philips, "The Cultural Revolution: All You Need to Know about China's Political Convulsion," *Guardian*, May 10, 2016, https://www.theguardian.com/world/2016/may/11/the-cultural-revolution-50-years-on-all-you-need-to-know-about-chinas-political-convulsion.

5 "Everywhere a Battlefield," Red Guards Austin, Aug. 27, 2017, https://redguardsaustin.wordpress.com/2017/08/27/everywhere-a-battlefield/.

6 Amy Chozick, "Hilary Clinton Calls Many Trump Backers 'Deplorables and G.O.P. Pounces," *New York Times*, Sept. 10, 2016,

http://www.nytimes.com/2016/09/11/us/politics/hillary-clinton
-basket-of-deplorables.html.

7   Anna Hopkins and Cheyenne Roundtree, "Majority of 230
    Protestors Arrested on Inauguration Day Will Face 10 Years in
    Prison and $25k in Fines as U.S. Attorney Says They Will Be
    Charged with Felony Rioting," *Daily News*, Jan. 21, 2017, http://
    www.dailymail.co.uk/news/article-4144360/Anti-Trump
    -protesters-face-10-years-prison.html.

8   Madison Park and Kyung Lah, "Berkeley Protests of
    Yiannopoulos Caused $10,000 in Damage," *CNN*, Feb. 2, 2017,
    http://www.cnn.com/2017/02/01/us/milo-yiannopoulos
    -berkeley/index.html.

9   Katie Mettler, "Portland Rose Parade Cancelled after 'Antifascists'
    Threaten GOP Marchers," *Washington Post*, April 27, 2017, https://
    www.washingtonpost.com/news/morning-mix/wp/2017/04/27/
    portland-rose-parade-canceled-after-antifascists-threaten-gop
    -marchers/?utm_term=.c3b23359bec7.

10 Patrick May, "Who's behind This Weekend's Right-Wing Rally
    at Crissy Field?" *Mercury News*, Aug. 23, 2017, http://www
    .mercurynews.com/2017/08/23/whos-behind-this-weekends
    -right-wing-rally-at-crissy-field/.

11 Kyle Swenson, "Black-Clad Antifa Members Attack Peaceful
    Right-Wing Demonstrators in Berkeley," *Washington Post*, Aug.
    28, 2017, https://www.washingtonpost.com/news/morning
    -mix/wp/2017/08/28/black-clad-antifa-attack-right-wing
    -demonstrators-in-berkeley/?utm_term=.d933be9e3aaf.

12 "Part I: Undercover Investigation Exposes Groups Plotting
    Criminal Activity at Trump Inauguration," YouTube video,
    posted by "veritasvisuals," the Veritas Project, Jan. 16, 2017,
    https://www.youtube.com/watch?v=MHZSfhd1X_8; and
    "Part II: New Investigation Uncovers Plot to Chain the Trains &
    Shut down Dc during Inauguration," YouTube video, posted by
    "veritasvisuals," the Veritas Project, Jan. 17, 2017, https://www
    .youtube.com/watch?v=xIjbkYLI1nY.

13 "Communist Thugs, Not Students Brought Mayhem at Berkeley,"
    GlennBeck, April 25, 2017, http://www.glennbeck.com/2017/
    04/25/Communist-thugs-not-students-brought-mayhem-at
    -berkeley/.

14   German Lopez, "The Debate over Punching White Nationalist Richard Spencer in the Face Explained," Vox, Jan. 26, 2017, https://www.vox.com/identities/2017/1/26/14369388/richard -spencer-punched-alt-right-trump.

15   German Lopez, "News Organizations Are Telling Writers to Be Clear That the Alt-Right Is a Racist Movement," Vox, Dec. 2, 2016, https://www.vox.com/policy-and-politics/2016/12/2/13818400/ alt-right-racist-style.

16   John Daniszewski, "Writing about the 'Alt-Right,'" *Definitive Source* (blog), Nov. 28, 2016, https://blog.ap.org/behind-the -news/writing-about-the-alt-right.

17   John Daniszewski, "How to Describe Extremists Who Rallied in Charlottesville," *Definitive Source* (blog), Aug. 15, 2017, https:// blog.ap.org/behind-the-news/how-to-describe-extremists-who -rallied-in-charlottesville.

18   Newt Gingrich, "Why Doesn't the Media Condemn Left-Wing Violence?" *Fox News*, Aug. 31, 2017, http://www.foxnews.com/ opinion/2017/08/31/newt-gingrich-why-doesnt-media-condemn -leftwing-violence.html.

Chapter 11

1   Edward L. Bernays, *Propaganda* (New York: Horace Liveright, 1928).

2   Ion Mihai Pacepa and Ronald J. Rychlak, *Disinformation: Former Spy Chief Reveals Secret Strategies for Undermining Freedom, Attacking Religion, and Promoting Terrorism* (Washington, DC: WND Books, 2013), 298–99.

3   Debra Heine, "Sen. Feinstein: No Evidence of Russian Collusion with Trump Campaign at This Time," PJ Media, May 4, 2017, https://pjmedia.com/trending/2017/05/04/sen-feinstein-no -evidence-of-russian-collusion-with-trump-campaign-at-this -time/.

4   Todd Shepherd, "James Clapper: Still No Evidence of Russian Collusion with Trump Campaign," *Washington Examiner*, May 8, 2017, http://www.washingtonexaminer.com/james-clapper-still -no-evidence-of-any-russian-collusion-with-trump-campaign/ article/2622452.

5   Joe Concha, "Dershowitz Slams New York Times Op-Ed for Broaching Trump Jr. Treason Charge," *Hill*, Jan. 12, 2017, http://

thehill.com/homenews/media/341703-dershowitz-slams-new
-york-times-op-ed-for-broaching-trump-jr-treason-charge.

6 Kailani Koenig, "Rep. Schiff: 'Circumstantial Evidence of
Collusion' between Trump and Russia," *NBC News*, March 19,
2017, https://www.nbcnews.com/politics/politics-news/schiff
-defends-committee-examining-russia-trump-connections
-n735391.

7 Karoun Bemirjian, "House Intelligence Chairman Devin Nunes
Recuses Himself from Russia Probe," *Washington Post*, April 6,
2017, https://www.washingtonpost.com/powerpost/house
-intelligence-chairman-devin-nunes-recuses-himself-from-russia
-probe/2017/04/06/8122b5bc-1ad2-11e7-855e-4824bbb5d748
_story.html?utm_term=.0d94c80f3138.

8 "'Wag the Dog' Back in Spotlight," *CNN Politics*, Aug. 21, 1998,
http://edition.cnn.com/ALLPOLITICS/1998/08/21/wag.the.dog/.

9 Stephen Dinan, "Federal Workers Hit Record Number, but
Growth Slows under Obama," *Washington Times*, Feb. 9, 2016,
http://www.washingtontimes.com/news/2016/feb/9/federal
-workers-hit-record-number-but-growth-slows/.

10 Clyde Wayne Crews Jr., "Obama's Legacy: 2016 Ends with a
Record-Shattering Regulatory Rulebook," *Forbes*, Dec. 30,
2016, https://www.forbes.com/sites/waynecrews/2016/12/30/
obamas-legacy-2016-ends-with-a-record-shattering-regulatory
-rulebook/#712927f01398.

Chapter 12

1 Ronald D. Rotunda, "Can Trump Be Indicted? Are Sitting
Presidents Immune from Prosecution?" *Newsweek*, Aug. 15, 2017,
http://www.newsweek.com/can-trump-be-indicted-are-sitting
-presidents-immune-prosecution-650484.

2 Ion Mihai Pacepa and Ronald J. Rychlak, *Disinformation: Former
Spy Chief Reveals Secret Strategies for Undermining Freedom, Attacking
Religion, and Promoting Terrorism* (Washington, DC: WND Books,
2013), 296.

3 US Department of Justice, Office of Public Affairs, "HSBC
Holdings Plc. and HSBC Bank USA N.A. Admit to Anti-Money
Laundering and Sanctions Violations, Forfeit $1.256 Billion in
Deferred Prosecution Agreement," press release, Dec. 11, 2012,
https://www.justice.gov/opa/pr/hsbc-holdings-plc-and-hsbc

-bank-usa-na-admit-anti-money-laundering-and-sanctions -violations.

4   Tyler Durden, "HSBC Bank: Secret Origins to Laundering the World's Drug Money," ZeroHedge, Feb. 16, 2015, http://www .zerohedge.com/news/2015-02-16/hsbc-bank-secret-origins -laundering-worlds-drug-money.

5   Nafeez Ahmed, "Death, Drugs, and HSBC: Fraudulent Blood Money Makes the World Go Round," Insurge Intelligence, March 2, 2015, https://medium.com/insurge-intelligence/death -drugs-and-hsbc-355ed9ef5316.

6   Dean Henderson, *Big Oil and Their Bankers in the Persian Gulf: Four Horsemen, Eight Families, and Their Global Intelligence, Narcotics, and Terror Network*, 3rd ed. (Bridger House, 2010).

7   Peter Dale Scott, *The American Deep State: Big Money, Big Oil, and the Struggle for U.S. Democracy*, updated ed. (Lanham, MD: Rowman & Littlefield, 2017).

8   Ahmed, "Death, Drugs, and HSBC."

9   Matt Taibbi, "Death, Drugs and HSBC: How HSBC Hooked Up with Drug Traffickers and Terrorists. And Got Away with It," *Rolling Stone*, Feb. 14, 2013, http://www.rollingstone.com/ politics/news/gangster-bankers-too-big-to-jail-20130214.

10   Carol D. Leonnig, Ashley Parker, Rosalind S. Helderman, and Tom Hamburger, "Trump Team Seeks to Control, Block Mueller's Russia Investigation," *Washington Post*, July 21, 2017, https://www .washingtonpost.com/politics/trumps-lawyers-seek-to-undercut -muellers-russia-investigation/2017/07/20/232ebf2c-6d71-11e7 -b9e2-2056c768a7e5_story.html?utm_term=.4c1aeccebf31.

11   Sidney Powell, *Licensed to Lie: Exposing Corruption in the Department of Justice* (Dallas, TX: Brown Books, 2014).

12   Ibid.

Conclusion

1   US Department of the Treasury, "Announcement of Additional Treasury Sanctions on Russian Government Officials and Entities," press release, April 28, 2014, https://www.treasury.gov/ press-center/press-releases/Pages/jl2369.aspx.

2   "Ukraine-Related Sanctions," Sullivan & Cromwell LLP, May 2, 2014, https://www.sullcrom.com/siteFiles/Publications/SC _Publication_Ukraine_Related_Sanctions_5_02_14.pdf.

3   Gerald Traufetter and Matthias Schepp, "Russia Didn't Initiate
    the Ukraine Crisis," *Der Spiegel*, Sept. 2, 2014, http://www.spiegel
    .de/international/business/rosneft-head-igor-sechin-speaks
    -about-sanctions-and-ukraine-a-989267.html.

4   "1950: McCarthy Says Communists Are in State Department,"
    History Channel, 2009, "This Day in History, Feb. 9," http://www
    .history.com/this-day-in-history/mccarthy-says-communists-are
    -in-state-department.

5   Alexander Bratersky, "Zbigniew Brzezinski: Russia Should Form a
    Closer Union with U.S. and China," Russia Beyond, April 7, 2017,
    https://www.rbth.com/international/2017/04/07/zbigniew
    -brzezinski-russia-should-form-a-closer-union-with-us-and
    -china_737177.

6   Maureen Dowd, "Jimmy Carter Lusts for a Trump Posting," *New
    York Times*, Oct. 21, 2017, https://www.nytimes.com/2017/10/21/
    opinion/sunday/jimmy-carter-lusts-trump-posting.html?_r=0.

7   Jerome R. Corsi, "Tech Giants to Senate: Russia Didn't Influence
    2016 Election," Infowars, Oct. 31, 2017, https://www.infowars
    .com/tech-giants-to-senate-russia-didnt-influence-2016
    -election/.

8   Testimony of Colin Stretch, General Counsel, Facebook, US
    Senate Judiciary Subcommittee on Crime and Terrorism, Oct. 31,
    2017, https://www.judiciary.senate.gov/imo/media/doc/10-31-17
    %20Stretch%20Testimony.pdf.

9   Testimony of Sean J. Edgett, Acting General Counsel, Twitter
    Inc., US Senate Judiciary Subcommittee on Crime and Terrorism,
    Oct. 31, 2017, https://www.judiciary.senate.gov/imo/media/doc/
    10-31-17%20Edgett%20Testimony.pdf.

10 Testimony of Richard Salgado, Senior Counsel, Law Enforcement
    and Information Security, Google, US Senate Judiciary
    Subcommittee on Crime and Terrorism, hearing on "Extremist
    Content and Russian Information Online: Working with Tech to
    Find Solutions," Oct. 31, 2017, https://www.judiciary.senate.gov/
    imo/media/doc/10-31-17%20Salgado%20Testimony.pdf.

Index

More Books From Humanix:

Simple **Heart Test**

Powered by Newsmaxhealth.com

FACT:

▸ Nearly half of those who die from heart attacks each year never showed prior symptoms of heart disease.

▸ If you suffer cardiac arrest outside of a hospital, you have just a 7% chance of survival.

Don't be caught off guard. Know your risk now.

TAKE THE TEST NOW ...

Renowned cardiologist **Dr. Chauncey Crandall** has partnered with **Newsmaxhealth.com** to create a simple, easy-to-complete, online test that will help you understand your heart attack risk factors. Dr. Crandall is the author of the #1 best-seller *The Simple Heart Cure: The 90-Day Program to Stop and Reverse Heart Disease.*

Take Dr. Crandall's Simple Heart Test — it takes just 2 minutes or less to complete — it could save your life!

Discover your risk now.

- **Where you score on our unique heart disease risk scale**
- **Which of your lifestyle habits really protect your heart**
- **The true role your height and weight play in heart attack risk**
- Little-known conditions that impact heart health
- **Plus much more!**

SimpleHeartTest.com/deep